Contents

Preface

We have worked together for more than 10 years, leading God's people to experience life transformation through worship. Before that, each of us had WORSHIP at the heart of our ministries.

So WORSHIP has rung through our lives in ministry for more than 40 years. Before that, both of us grew up in families devoted to true biblical worship. Our own lives bear witness that worship has been life transforming for each of us and our families.

Both of us have become deeply concerned, in an ever-increasing manner, at how disoriented to true worship God's people are becoming. This is increasingly evident in the growing pain and brokenness in the churches. And as unbelievable as it may seem, today much of the bewilderment and fracturing of God's people is centered in WORSHIP, or worship style. The enemy of God and His people is destroying the work of God at its heart—WORSHIP!

When we were asked if we would consider writing a book together on WORSHIP, we were immediately full of gratitude. But we also asked, "Why us?" But we have been assured by God and many others, "Why not you?" So we have asked many people to pray with us as we wrote, that God would guide us into all truth and grant us the ability to communicate it in writing.

We release this study to God and to you, His people who will be studying it, with the earnest prayer that God will be glorified. We pray that His people once again will experience individually and together the fullness of God and His working, through WORSHIP. We also covenant to pray for all who will read and study this book! May our God receive all the glory!

Writers

Henry Blackaby

Henry Blackaby has spent his life in ministry. He has served as a music director, Christian education director, and senior pastor in churches in California and Canada. His first church assignment was in 1958. Following his local church ministry, Dr. Blackaby became a college president, a missionary, and an executive in the Southern Baptist Convention.

Blackaby served at the North American Mission Board in Alpharetta, Georgia, as special assistant to the president. Through the office of Revival and Spiritual Awakening, he provided leadership to thousands of pastors and laymen across North America. He also formerly served as special assistant to the presidents of the International Mission Board and LifeWay Christian Resources of the Southern Baptist Convention.

In the early 90s, Blackaby became one of North America's bestselling Christian authors, committing the rest of his life to helping people know and experience God. The author of more than a dozen books, including *Experiencing God: Knowing and Doing the Will of God*, he is a graduate of the University of British Columbia, Vancouver, Canada. He has completed his Th.M. degree from Golden Gate Baptist Theological Seminary. He also holds three honorary doctorate degrees.

Henry Blackaby and his wife, Marilynn, have five married children. He currently serves as the president of Henry Blackaby Ministries.

For further information about Henry Blackaby and his ministry please contact: Henry Blackaby Ministries, P.O. Box 161228, Atlanta, GA 30321; www.henryblackaby.com.

Ron Owens

Born in Nova Scotia, the son of missionaries, Ron Owens spent his teenage years in Switzerland. He came to faith in Christ at age 16 in Schwennigen, Germany.

Ron studied and holds degrees from Ecole Lemania and Ecole de Commerce, both in Lausanne. He holds bachelor of theology and music degrees, and he has studied at the Eastman School of Music, Rochester, New York, where he met his wife Patricia.

Ron and Patricia have ministered through music in many areas of the world—composing, publishing, and recording. Their music has been translated into many languages. Ron has also authored *Return to Worship*, published by Broadman & Holman.

From 1983-1990, Owens was associated in ministry with Dr. Stephen F. Olford. In 1990, he became associate to Henry Blackaby at the North American Mission Board, where he served for 10 years.

In 1998, Ron and Patricia became worship and music consultants for the International Mission Board of the Southern Baptist Convention. They presently minister together in conferences and seminars in Southern Baptist and other evangelical churches, missionary training sessions, seminaries, and colleges in the United States and in many countries around the world, with special interest in Russia.

Ron and Patricia have one married son.

Introduction

Any study of worship is incomplete without a life-action response. In this interactive study we present a process where God brings you face-to-face with His truth. Then He will guide you to an interaction with that truth. This is not a study for the reader to "run through" to see how enjoyable it might be; but it is to bring the pastor, staff, church leaders, and congregation to a mutual conviction regarding what worship is as God has revealed it in His Word. The purpose of this study is to help a church corporately come to unity of heart and life in their understanding and experience of God's requirements and standards for worship.

The question is often asked, what advantage is there in my participating in an interactive study over my simply reading a book on the subject? These two approaches to learning have several distinct differences, and we believe that in dealing with this particular subject of worship, about which so much has been written and around which there is so much controversy, there are definite advantages to looking for answers in the context of an interactive study with others.

Many people today are interested in reading books on worship that others have written and thus letting others do their thinking for them. Sometimes these books do impact the life of the reader. But often little lasting change is brought about because the reader did not let the Holy Spirit guide them in truth as they studied the Scriptures for themselves. Therefore, reading and studying with others not only leaves a deeper impact but also brings alongside the reader an accountability to implement into life what was learned from those with whom they studied.

We live in a generation that does not want to get too involved or have to think too deeply. This is especially true when it requires interacting with others to let God guide them together. Yet basic to any relationship with truth, interaction with God's people—with an open

Bible, with the Holy Spirit teaching them—is vital and life transforming.

Our relationship with God is one of deep interaction. The fellowship for which we were created was built on interdependence. God does not function in one's life without interaction. To say you believe something without an equivalent action—response with the truth—is what James called dead faith. Faith without action and response is useless in God's sight (Jas. 2:20). Abraham's faith was justified by his actions, in response to who he knew God to be. "Faith was working with his works, and as a result of the works, faith was perfected" (Jas. 2:22, NASB). We can tell God that we are ready to offer our Isaac on the altar, but it is not until we get to the point of actually offering him that faith is completed, and worship also is completed.

Being willing to read about worship but not willing to have an interactive involvement in true worship is no different from our saying that we are ready to offer our Isaac on the altar while not being willing to act on it. To God worship is so vital that to fail to experience genuine worship is fatal. Yet it is possible to go through life thinking we have worshiped without ever having done so.

Knowing God's standards, and responding in loving obedience is of fundamental importance, because lives are then transformed. It is in true worship that God responds to what we have done, according to His pattern. God reveals and sets the standard, and His work is accomplished in the life of the worshiper as the worshiper responds to what God has required. Genuine worship is always transformational, but we cannot transform our own lives. That is God's work. This amazing transformation comes preeminently in worship.

Romans 12:1-2 clearly states that the kind of worship God is looking for and accepts is the presenting of our bodies as living sacrifices, which is our "spiritual act of worship" (v. 1). But then the second verse comes into play: "Be not conformed to this world but be . . . transformed by the renewing of your mind" (KJV). The connection between verse 1, the "positive" aspect, and verse 2, the "negative," is often overlooked, yet we cannot fulfill the requirement of verse 1 without the application of verse 2 to our lives.

Only one kind of worship is acceptable to God. We must not let the world draw us away from His standard. We must not allow the world to entice us to pursue that which appeals only to the flesh. If we do, not only will we not be offering God the worship He requires, but we will also never know God's "good, and acceptable, and perfect will" (v. 2, KJV). In this study we are going to give biblical and practical help for God's people to be able to discern what is truth and to withstand

To God worship is so vital that to fail to experience genuine worship is fatal.

Genuine worship is always transformational.

This amazing transformation comes preeminently in worship.

the temptation to become like the world in this crucial area of worship.

Any departure from God's standard is sin, and sin is fatal. Sin is missing the mark or simply not meeting God's standard. This is as true in our worship as in any other area of life. Sin is any departure from the ideal, and when we do not deal with sin, it results in death. Jesus said, "The Spirit gives life; the flesh counts for nothing. The words I have spoken to you are spirit and they are life" (John 6:63).

To depart from God's Word or standard in worship is fatal, no matter how innovative we may think we are. To experiment for experiment's sake is dangerous. The obsession with being creative or innovative can lead to substituting for the real. In worship the criterion is never how people are responding to us but how God is responding to us. King Saul led in worship, in the offering of sacrifices, and all the people participated. But the offering was rejected by God. To the casual observer everything looked great. Solomon and Elijah, however, did everything God had commanded them (2 Chron. 1–7; 1 Kings 18). Their concern was not with how the people responded but with how God was going to respond. In each case the fire fell! If the fire had not fallen, they would have known that what they had done was unacceptable to God. Where there is no fire, there has not been an acceptable offering. The people may enjoy themselves and even shout, "Amen!" Even when there is no "fire," the worship leaders often assure the congregation that they have really worshiped. The issue in worship is not how much we can orchestrate excitement, but rather, has the "fire" fallen? Is it obvious to all that God is present in our worship? Are the worshipers' lives being transformed by their encounter with God?

Both in the writing and in the studying of this material, we all are most dependent on the enabling, the inspiration, the teaching and illuminating work of the Holy Spirit. In John 16:13, we read that "when he, the Spirit of truth, comes, he will guide you into all truth." In John 16:8, Jesus said: "He will convict the world of guilt in regard to sin [where we are missing the mark in our worship] and righteousness [He will show us what is right] and judgment [we will be held accountable for how we have handled the truth that has been revealed to us]."

In this study you will find extensive use of Scripture. The only sure place to find God's standard is in His Word because that is where He speaks. We will be doing a careful study of key Scriptures that pertain to these standards. And it is interesting to note that even John (Rev. 22:18-19) realized that when God reveals Himself and His will in His Word, no one should alter it.

Our ultimate desire for this interactive study is that it will be a tool,

In worship the criterion is never how people are responding to us but how God is responding to us.

a resource, and an aid for you to encounter God in worship. We have not written as ones who give all the answers but as guides to lead toward the light where the answers can be found. We have not tried to do all the thinking for you, but pray that this will help and encourage you in your own personal and corporate search for all that God wants to show you. The most significant thing is what the Holy Spirit reveals through the Word of God to the people of God. Our desire is to point you to the right "door," knowing that those who enter that door will meet the truth and the truth will make them free (John 8:31-32,36).

Nothing is higher on God's agenda for Himself and for His people than true worship.

One final word by way of introduction. Nothing is higher on God's agenda for Himself and for His people than true worship. It is, therefore, also true that nothing is higher on the agenda of Satan, the enemy of God than to: (1) deceive God's people in worship (he is called a deceiver in Rev. 12:9; 20:10); (2) create substitutes for true worship; and (3) distort and change true worship. From Jesus' example, when Satan tempted Him, the only sure way of dealing with this deception, is Scripture (Matt. 4:1-11).

Some of Satan's deceptions may include: the tradition of men, the words of men, the persuasions of men, the pleading of men, the perpetuated fads of men, or even the allure of popularity with men (i.e. numbers, crowds, etc.).

God has always guided His people by a clear Word of revelation. Satan has always twisted and distorted God's Word. God's Holy Spirit is always present in His people to correct all that they are confronting and bring everything into harmony with God's Word. So God's people proceed in the confidence that God will guide them into all truth and the truth will continuously set them free (John 8:31-32,36).

What God Did in Creation

As far back as God has allowed us to look into eternity past, we find worship. Even before He created our world there was worship. In fact, it was over worship that the archangel Lucifer led his rebellion in heaven when he tried to overthrow the throne (Isa. 14:12-14). A large part of heaven's angelic host joined him in his attempt to unseat God, so that Lucifer could be the object of heaven's worship. They were, of course, eventually defeated and cast out of heaven, but the attempt to dethrone God did not end there. From that point on, Satan and his demons have been working to secure the worship of God's creation. That is at the heart of the conflict that Satan has with God. He is fighting for the allegiance, or the worship, of humankind.

In the very act of creation itself, God was expressing His love. He created Adam and Eve for Himself, and He gave them all that they would ever need. Not one thing was missing, and everything He provided was perfect. Adam and Eve, in turn, were to love God, commune with Him, worship Him, and enjoy Him forever!

Have you observed that God has placed into human nature the need and the desire to worship? Think about it. If we were to go to the most remote area on earth and watch the most primitive tribe, we would find those people worshiping some god or gods. Why is this? The answer would appear to be simply that this is the way God created us.

Everyone of us is a worshiper of something or someone. That which is most important to us, which we value the most, is the object of our worship, and it is to that (or that one) we will bow, giving our allegiance, our interest, our time, and our affection. Jesus said: "For where your treasure is, there your heart will be also" (Matt. 6:21). Yes, everyone worships something or someone. If I could be an unseen observer of your life for the period of a month, what or whom do you think I would conclude is the object of your worship? More importantly, what

Key Verse

"A time is coming and has now come when true worshipers will worship the Father in spirit and truth, for they are the kind of worshipers the Father seeks. God is spirit, and his worshipers must worship in spirit and in truth."

— John 4:23-24

This Week's Lessons

1. What Does It Mean to Worship God in Spirit?

2. What Does It Mean to Worship God in Truth?

3. What Did God Require of Old Testament Worshipers?

4. What Does God Require of New Testament Worshipers?

5. What Is the Relationship Between Worship and the New Birth?

Worship is the response of an adoring heart to the magnificence of God. In the highest sense of the word, it is the occupation of the created with the Creator Himself. It is the pure joy of magnifying the One whose name is above every other name.

does your own honest reflection about your preferences and choices cause you to conclude is the object of your worship? Let this be a beginning point of evaluation as we consider this vital matter of worship.

In this unit we are going to be discussing what the Bible says about the worship God requires. We will look at both the Old and New Testaments, and one of our discoveries will be that it is not just worship the Father is seeking, but He is seeking a certain kind of worshiper, the kind He created humankind to be in the garden of Eden.

Day 1: What Does It Mean to Worship God in Spirit?

In Old Testament times, during King Solomon's reign, God chose to inhabit the temple, which was built in Jerusalem to honor Him. Solomon had received the details of the plans of the building from his father, David, who in turn had received the understanding of the plans from the Lord (1 Chron. 28:11-12,19). It was a building of majesty and beauty and God-given design, and God made it plain that this was the only place His people should go to worship Him.

In the encounter which Jesus had with the Samaritan woman near the village of Sycar, however, Jesus made a startling announcement. He told the woman, "A time is coming and has now come when the true worshipers will worship the Father in spirit . . ." (John 4:23). Jesus was announcing that matters of the exterior would become secondary and that matters of the interior were God's primary interest and requirement. He would be looking to see if worship comes from within our innermost being, our hearts.

This of course had always been the fundamental desire of God. David understood this as he penned his Psalms. Read Psalm 45:1 and Psalm 103:1. David felt a strong, personal response to who God is. How have you sensed God's desire for your worship? What have you felt like doing when you have experienced an incredible occasion of God's blessing?

_____

_____

_____

My heart is stirred by a noble theme as I recite my verses for the king; my tongue is the pen of a skillful writer.

— Psalm 45:1

Praise the Lord, O my soul; all my inmost being, praise his holy name.

— Psalm 103:1

When our Lord said to the Samaritan woman that "a time is coming and has now come when the true worshipers will worship the Father in spirit," He was making a direct reference to our inner being, or our human spirit. He told her that the place of worship would no longer have to be the temple in Jerusalem but that wherever God's children gathered they could offer the Father the worship He was seeking as long as it was "in spirit." It would flow from their inner being.

The apostle Paul knew what God wanted. He understood that our worship "of service" also came from the inside. He said, "God, whom I serve in my spirit in the preaching of the gospel of His Son" (Rom. 1:9, NASB). The word *serve* is a Greek word (*latreuo*) which can also be translated "worship." In other words Paul's ministry itself was a form of worship. It was not something he did because he felt he had to; rather, it was something he did out of love for his Lord.

Worship comes from within. God is not at all impressed with outward expressions of worship that do not come from our hearts, no matter how excellent we may think they are. God hears and receives only what is offered to Him in spirit. Jesus noted this with great sorrow in His heart when He said: "These people honor me with their lips, but their hearts are far from me. They worship me in vain" (Matt. 15:8-9).

Read Romans 1:9. Read it again, this time replacing the word *serve* with *worship*. Evaluate yourself: do you actively worship God with your whole heart as you preach or talk about, teach or live out, the truth of the gospel, in your daily life? Explain.

_____

_____

_____

_____

If we are to worship "in spirit," four fundamental things will be true about us.

1. We will be born of the Spirit. When Jesus had His important conversation with the Pharisee, Nicodemus, He informed him that he "must be born again" (John 3:7). He explained that "that which is born of the Spirit is spirit" (John 3:6, KJV). While human life reproduces human life, it takes the Spirit of God to breathe divine life into the spirit of man. Until we are born of the Spirit of God, our human spirits are dead toward God. When we come to Christ in faith, drawn to Him by the Holy Spirit, God does His miracle work within us, and we are birthed into His kingdom, and our spirits are alive to God.

2. We will recognize the importance of the Holy Spirit's working in our lives and yield our hearts to His control because He is the One who sparks worship for God in our spirit. How does He do this? Jesus told His disciples that "When he, the Spirit of truth, comes, . . . he will bring glory to me by taking from what is mine and making it known to you" (John 16:13-14). That means the Holy Spirit takes some truth concerning the person of Christ, or the promises of our Lord, or the deeds of our Savior, or the exalted position of our Great High Priest and makes

God, whom I serve with my whole heart in preaching the gospel of his Son, is my witness how constantly I remember you.

— Romans 1:9

them so personally understood and precious that it ignites within us an "Amen," or, a "Thank you, Lord!" or, "How wonderful you are, Lord Jesus!" He is the One who triggers this adoration and praise in our spirit.

3. *We will respond to the Holy Spirit's conviction and correction, maintaining a repentant and contrite heart toward God.* In Psalm 66:18, NASB, the psalmist expresses a truth which is often passed over lightly. He said: "If I regard [cherish] wickedness in my heart, the Lord will not hear." Sin is always an obstacle to fellowship with God. God will not receive our words of adoration, our praise or petitions if He detects that our spirits are polluted with sins we haven't confessed to Him and of which we have not repented (turned away).

Yet another one of the Holy Spirit's assignments is to convict us when we sin so that we can recognize that we have offended God. He will bring to our remembrance the commands of our Lord and show us where we have disobeyed Him. Then we can confess our sins to God, asking Him to cleanse us from our sins. Then our fellowship with the Lord is restored.

4. *Our focus will be on God.* God is both the subject and the object of worship. In other words worship is an encounter with God where He turns everything toward Himself because He is our life. It is easy to lose this focus, however, especially when the worship we are offering to God is being done through the vehicle of music. Our emotions can be so deeply affected by music that without realizing it the music itself can end up being what is most important to us. Some people actually go to church more for the music than anything else.

Many, when they think of worship, think exclusively of music. A large percentage of the evangelical world today, if asked what kind of worship they have in their churches, would answer in a musical context, such as, "We have contemporary worship," or, "We have traditional worship," or, "We have blended worship," all the time thinking only of the style of music used.

Many today think that worship is music, that music is worship, and some actually worship music. Because of the innate power it has to sway our emotions, we must be careful that the music itself not become the focus of our worship.

It is also easy for people to become the center of attention, the focus of a service. It is for this reason that there is no place for entertainment in worship. Whenever a congregation becomes more impressed with a preacher, a worship leader or minister of music, a choir, or a soloist than with God, there results a divided heart on the part of a congregation; a divided focus.

Yet another one of the Holy Spirit's assignments is to convict us when we sin so that we can recognize that we have offended God.

The psalmist said: "Teach me your way, O Lord, and I will walk in your truth; give me an undivided heart, that I may fear your name" (Ps. 86:11) Worship that is offered "in spirit" will be focused exclusively on God. Check your God focus as you rate from 1-10, (1 being lowest) how aware you are of the following as you worship:

Being reborn into the kingdom of God is a miracle I remember in personal or corporate worship.

1 _____ 10

The Holy Spirit triggers in me adoration and praise of God when I worship.

1 _____ 10

When I worship, I am convicted of my sin so that I can confess, repent, and be restored to fellowship with God.

1 _____ 10

My desire to worship God is stronger than my desire to be pleased by the music or worship leaders.

1 _____ 10

Teach me your way,
O Lord, and I will walk
in your truth; give me an
undivided heart, that I
may fear your name.
— Psalm 86:11

16

Day 2: What Does It Mean to Worship God in Truth?

What does it mean to worship in "truth?" A good beginning point in looking for an answer to what our Lord meant when He said that the Father was looking for those who would worship Him in truth is to understand that truth is fundamentally a person, and this person is the Lord Jesus Christ Himself. He is the One who says, as our verse for the day reads: "I am the way and the truth and the life" (John 14:6). We can paraphrase the remainder of that verse by saying, "no one can worship the Father except through Me."

Worship under the New Covenant is always through Christ, in Christ, and for Christ. Our Lord is the embodiment of truth. Another way of putting it is to say that He is the incarnation of truth. Anything called truth that in any way contradicts who He is, His character, or what He has said is not truth.

When Jesus said that the Father looks for those who are worshiping Him "in truth," He is forever tying truth to worship and worship to truth. He is saying that the mind is engaged in the kind of worship God wants. He is saying that you cannot separate true worship from "truth." Worship is more than an emotional exercise. He is saying that when we attend a worship service we don't leave our minds at the door. The foundation of true worship is the Word of God.

To worship "in truth" means that our worship will be based on God's revelation to us in His Word. It will be consistent with how He has revealed Himself. The only standard, or plumb line, that stretches unchanged throughout history is the standard of God's Word. In it we have the revelation of God's character—who He is and what He requires. Our perception of God, what we understand Him to be, will be directly reflected in how we worship Him. If we view Him, as one contemporary song describes Him; "He's just like me, He's just like me," then just about anything goes. How thankful I am that He is not, or ever was, like me. He became flesh, but never for a moment did He become any less divine. Fundamental to offering God acceptable worship is having a correct view of Him.

A magnificent picture of the apostle Paul's view of God is found in 1 Timothy 1:17, KJV, as he writes his first letter to his son in the ministry: "Now unto the King eternal, immortal, invisible, the only wise God, be honour and glory for ever and ever. Amen." Every letter Paul wrote, every prayer he prayed, and every sermon he preached were shaped by his view of God. The God he served and worshiped was the God who provided a lamb for Abraham on Mount Moriah. This was

"I am the way and the truth and the life. No one comes to the Father except through me."
— John 14:6

Our Lord is the . . . incarnation of truth. Anything called truth that in any way contradicts who He is, His character, or what He has said is not truth.

the God Jacob encountered in a night of wrestling; afterward he bore a limp and a new name for the rest of his life. This was the God who revealed Himself to Moses at the burning bush, who delivered His people from Egyptian slavery, and who declared to them on Mount Sinai that He was the only God. They were never to bow down to any other.

Read what the psalmist said in Psalm 104:1, then respond to this: Pictures help us focus and explain what we believe. Make a descriptive statement, or draw a symbol or scene that describes God's honor or majesty. Show and explain your description to someone.

O Lord my God, you are very greatp; you are clothed with splendor and majesty.

— Psalm 104:1

_____

_____

_____

_____

The apostle Paul instructed believers to think on whatever was noble, right, pure, lovely, admirable, excellent, and praiseworthy (Phil. 4:8). Why is it important that we do this? Because it is the Word of God. It is the truth about who He is, and the Holy Spirit takes this and shapes us into the kind of worshiper the Father is seeking.

Do you remember what Jesus prayed to His Father in John 17:17? He said, "Sanctify them by the truth; your word is truth." In Ephesians 5:26, we read how the church is made holy and clean "by the washing with water through the word." If we are to worship "in truth," we will need the truth to wash our hearts. Washing and worshiping cannot be separated.

To worship in "truth" also means that the preaching and reading of God's Word will be indispensable in our worship services. As worshipers, we want to hear from God. Those who say that they enjoyed a worship service but could have done without the preaching are seriously disoriented to what worship is. If worship is a response to God's revelation, then the reading and expounding of His Word is imperative.

One of the main reasons the early church gathered together for worship was to be taught the apostles' doctrine. In Nehemiah 8, we see how God's Word motivated the people to worship God. After Ezra had read the writings of Moses, the people "lifted their hands and responded,

'Amen! Amen!' Then they bowed down and worshiped the Lord with their faces to the ground" (v. 6).

When you hear the Word of God preached or read, what kind of response do you make? Do you allow it to change you?

_____

_____

_____

_____

How does this affect your understanding of what it means "to worship in truth"?

_____

_____

_____

_____

If worship is a response to God's revelation, then the reading and expounding of His Word is imperative.

To worship in "truth" also means that we as individual worshipers will study God's Word. We will want to grow in our understanding of the God we worship because the measure in which we know God is the measure in which we will be able to worship Him. In Psalm 119, the psalmist writes of the importance of God's Word in his life. In verse 11, he says, "I have hidden your word in my heart that I might not sin against you." He says in verse 18, "Open my eyes that I may see wonderful things in your law." This is the expression of a worshiper who understands the importance God's Word has in his offering to God worship that is "in truth." As individual worshipers we will not be satisfied with reading or hearing from God's Word one day a week but will want to meditate on it daily.

Read Psalm 119:18 once more, and think about the implications in your life of having your eyes opened to "wonderful things" in God's law. List some actions you could take now to obey God's law. List some sins that

Open my eyes that I may
see wonderful things in
your law.

— Psalm 119:18

the Word of God, hidden in your life, could prevent you from committing again.

_____

_____

_____

_____

Day 3: What Did God Require of Old Testament Worshipers?

What Worship Meant in the Old Testament

The first place we find the word *worship* mentioned in the Bible is in Genesis 22, and it is linked to two other words that are also first mentioned in this chapter. These words are *love* and *obedience*, and they are found in the context of God's testing of Abraham when He asked Abraham to sacrifice his son Isaac. These three words are inseparable. Why are they inseparable? Because the kind of worshipers God wants don't worship Him out of duty but out of love. We worship because we desire to be obedient to the One we love, the One who is worthy of our worship. Jesus said to His followers: "If you love Me, you will keep My commandments" (John 14:15, NASB). In other words, "If you love me, you will do what I say."

Write a statement in your own words of what God requires of those who worship in truth.

_____

_____

_____

Worship— The Hebrew word for worship used in Genesis 22 is the word *shachah*. Wherever we find it in Scripture, and it is used 170 times in the Old Testament, we have a picture of someone bowing, kneeling, stooping, or prostrating on the ground before God. In Old Testament days this was something that those who worshiped God did physically. But the true meaning of this word goes way beyond any outward expression of worship; it has to do preeminently with the heart. It is an inward attitude. It is not so much something we do as much as it is someone we are. In fact, the acceptance by God of what we do in worship depends on this attitude of heart.

In the first chapter of Isaiah, God's children were "doing" all the outward worship correctly, but because their hearts were not in it, God said, "When you spread out your hands in prayer, I will hide my eyes from you; even if you offer many prayers, I will not listen" (Isa. 1:15). In the Old Testament God required His people to have *shachah* hearts, for that is what worship means.

"But the Lord, who brought you up out of Egypt with mighty power and outstretched arm, is the one you must worship. To him you shall bow down and to him offer sacrifices."
— 2 Kings 17:36

Do you have a *shachah* heart? Explain your response.

_____

_____

_____

_____

Several other Old Testament passages that picture *shachah* hearts.

Exodus 4:29-31 — Even before they had been delivered from Egyptian bondage, the children of Israel "bowed down and worshiped" (v. 31) when Moses told them that God had heard their cries and was going to deliver them.

1 Chronicles 29:10-20 — At the end of David's reign as king and after the offerings had been received for the building of the temple that would be built by Solomon's son, David prays a prayer of thanksgiving and blessing for his people, after which "the congregation blessed the Lord God of their fathers, and bowed down their heads, and worshipped the Lord, and the king" (v. 20, KJV).

Nehemiah 8:5-6 — The response of the people when Ezra stood to read God's Word, after they had not heard it for so many years, was that they "bowed their heads, and worshipped the Lord with their faces to the ground (v. 6, KJV).

Psalm 95:6-7 — The Psalms are full of expressions of worship. "O come, let us worship and bow down: let us kneel before the Lord our maker" (v. 6, KJV).

All of these portray the kind of heart God desires in everyone who approaches Him in worship.

Love — As great as Abraham's love was for his son, Isaac, his love for God was greater. When asked which of the commandments was the greatest, Jesus answered: "You shall love the Lord your God with all your heart, and with all your soul, and with all your mind" (Matt. 22:37, NASB).

Is it love for God that motivates your worship? Sometimes people go to church for other reasons than a profound love for God. Wise are the Christians, who, from time to time, check up on what motivates them. In our Lord's letter to the Ephesian church in Revelation 2, He accused them of leaving their first love. They were doing a lot of good

Come, let us bow down in worship, let us kneel before the Lord our Maker.

— Psalm 95:6

things, and they were commended for these, but in God's sight they had begun neglecting that which was most important—loving Him supremely. He told them that unless they repented of their sin of loving other things more than Him, He would remove His light, His presence, from them. Are we motivated to worship God because of our love for Him?

Read Revelation 2:2-4. How could a group of believers, admirable in so many ways, manage to function without loving God and placing Him first?

_____

_____

_____

Obey—The picture we see of Abraham in Scripture is of one who is "on ready" to obey what God asks him to do. It was a lifestyle with him that began when God told him to leave his country and relatives and to start journeying to a place he had never heard of before (Gen. 12). He demonstrated one of the characteristics of a true worshiper, obedience. If we are not eager to obey what God asks us to do, we are not ready to worship. Obedience is central to worship.

What is the relationship between being willing to obey God and being able to worship God? Thinking back, what have you found your experience to be? Have there been times when you have been living in disobedience but have still tried to worship God?

_____

_____

Then, later on at Mt. Sinai, God laid down, in no uncertain terms, what His requirements and guidelines for worship would be. By His grace and mercy He had delivered His people from Egyptian slavery. It was nothing they had earned. He had chosen them, He had called them to Himself, and now He was telling them how they were to live within the freedom He had given them, more of what He expected worship of Him to be.

"I know your deeds, your hard work and your perseverance. I know that you cannot tolerate wicked men, that you have tested those who claim to be apostles but are not, and have found them false. You have persevered and have endured hardships for my name, and have not grown weary. Yet I hold this against you: You have forsaken your first love."

— Revelation 2:2-4

Just before He burned the commandments into stone tablets, He made this statement: "I am the Lord your God, who brought you out of Egypt, out of the land of slavery" (Ex. 20:2). This opening statement of self-identification would leave no question in the minds of His people as to who was speaking. "I am the Lord your God." This understanding of who He was would be foundational to everything else they would do.

There are many places in the Old Testament where God preceded what He was about to say to His people with these words because it seemed that they were forever forgetting who He really was. This lack of understanding was at the root of all their departures from Him. We have the same problem today.

Have you felt the impact of who God is, and has this kept you from departing from Him? Explain.

_____

_____

_____

What effect will being reminded of who God truly is have on your worship?

_____

_____

_____

On the heels of His giving them these guidelines, He instructs the Hebrew people to build a *place* for worship, a place where He would dwell. This place, the tabernacle, would be where He would establish His residence on earth.

The Place

The tabernacle was a rare and holy place. It was where He would dwell. It was where God's presence would dwell. It was where God would meet with His people and receive their sacrifices. This is where we first hear of God's plan to also live on earth. He said in Exodus 29:45, "I will dwell among the Israelites and be their God."

The "place" would be where they would relate in worship. In the introduction to this book we talked about the importance of interaction. God was forever establishing that interaction with Him was fundamental to worshiping Him. The tabernacle was to be the "meeting place," the place that was set apart for God and His people. There is no true worship without a relationship between the One being worshiped and the worshiper himself. Worship is a place of meeting, a time of interaction between God's people and the object of their worship, God Himself.

The Priests as Worship Leaders

In Leviticus 21:1,6, 8, "The Lord said to Moses, 'Speak to the priests, the sons of Aaron, and say to them: "They must be holy to their God and must not profane the name of their God. . . . Consider them holy, because I the Lord am holy—I who make you holy."'"

Just as the "place" was to be set apart, so were the ones assigned to lead the worship. In the Old Testament the worship leaders, the priests, were sanctified, washed with water (Ex. 29:4). This was a picture of the importance God placed on the worship leaders being morally acceptable to serve in this capacity. In Exodus 28:2, we read how even their garments were to be holy, or "set apart."

In what ways does God hold worship leaders to a higher standard in their service to Him?

_____

_____

_____

What impact does being set apart and clean from sin have on your readiness to be used by God?

_____

_____

_____

There is no true worship without a relationship between the One being worshiped and the worshiper himself. Worship is a place of meeting, a time of interaction between God's people and the object of their worship, God Himself.

The Levites as Musician Worship Leaders

The Levites were a part of the priesthood, and we find the same requirements that were made for the priests were made for the Levites who were in charge of the music. The worship of God was a serious matter, and the musician worship leaders were held to "God's standards" of behavior and service. They were to be "purified" (Num. 8:5-15). They were led through a ceremony of cleansing, just as were the pastor-priests.

The People

God also set standards for the people themselves. In fact, these standards were set on Mount Sinai when He gave them the Ten Commandments, as we have already studied today. The first four dealt specifically with their relationship to God in worship. Let's close our lesson today by looking briefly at the first commandment in light of what God required of Old Testament worshipers.

"You shall have no other gods before me" (Ex. 20:3). That's it! In other words, "Nothing is to be more important in your life than I am. You are free to worship and love Me with all your heart, soul, mind, and strength. You can go to any means to express this, and in return you will be the recipient of My love, grace, and provision. Just remember that 'I am your God.'" That is why, when Jesus was asked which was the greatest commandment, He quoted this one. It is foundational to all true worship; and when this one is broken, God pays no attention to what we offer Him. Martin Luther is purported to have said that if this is the greatest commandment, then the greatest sin is not to keep it.

Throughout the Old Testament the breaking of the first commandment evoked God's anger against His people more than anything else they did. When this one was broken, the breaking of the next three was soon to follow. His people would create idols, they would misuse His name, and they would begin to desecrate the Sabbath.

Read the excerpts from Exodus 20:3-8. Summarize the progression of disobedience that results from breaking one commandment.

_____

_____

_____

_____

"You shall have no other gods before me. You shall not make for yourself an idol in the form of anything. . . . You shall not misuse the name of the Lord your God. . . . Remember the Sabbath day by keeping it holy."

— Exodus 20:3-4,7-8

We may think that we are not guilty of breaking this commandment today because when we think of worshiping other gods our minds immediately think of the multitude of other deities people worship around the world, such as Buddha or Mohammed, yet this may be the one we most often break.

In Old Testament days, the idols a nation worshiped represented the values and belief system of that nation. Its idols were reflected in the way people lived—what they ate, how they dressed, and the music they enjoyed. God's people, the children of Israel, often became enamored with the cultures around them, and they were soon incorporating the gods of these cultures into their own worship. And when this happened, God became angry because with Him there can be no mixture or compromise. Either they worshiped Him exclusively, or they would come under His hand of discipline. And in the disciplining of His people, the nations around them would see that He was a holy God. They were His alone for His exclusive purposes. To interfere with this solitary relationship was fatal to God's people.

This was made clear in His words to the prophet Ezekiel: "Therefore say to the house of Israel, 'This is what the Sovereign Lord says: It is not for your sake, O house of Israel, that I am going to do these things, but for the sake of my holy name, which you have profaned among the nations where you have gone. I will show the holiness of my great name, which has been profaned among the nations. . . . Then the nations will know that I am the Lord, declares the Sovereign Lord, when I show myself holy through you before their eyes'" (Ezek. 36:22-23).

In Exodus 32:1-20, we have the story of the children of Israel getting restless and turning away from God when Moses did not return from his meeting with God on the mountain. When the golden calf had been molded out of the people's earrings, they began to worship the calf with music and behavior that was totally contrary to God's nature. It was the absolute antithesis of what was happening on the mountain. Where had they seen this behavior? Where had they heard this music? From the nations around them. In that moment they took on the sounds and the actions of that world.

What a contrast this is to the stand Daniel and the three young Hebrew men took, who found themselves in the midst of a heathen culture. They, however, refused to compromise. They could not become like the world around them. They could not bow down to the idol Nebuchadnezzar had built, for in so doing they would have renounced their covenant lifestyle, which represented the covenant God had made with His people. They would be breaking the commandment not to bow

"This is what the Sovereign Lord says: It is not for your sake, O house of Israel, that I am going to do these things, but for the sake of my holy name, which you have profaned among the nations where you have gone. I will show the holiness of my great name, which has been profaned among the nations. . . . Then the nations will know that I am the Lord, declares the Sovereign Lord, when I show myself holy through you before their eyes."

— Ezekiel 36:22-23

down to another god. They knew that if they did, they would be accepting and embracing the lifestyle of another god and culture.

How does this apply to us today? How committed are we to worshiping God alone? The lifestyles we choose reflect the god(s) we worship. When we worship the one true God, Yahweh, our way of living will be consistent with who He is and what He represents. We will find ourselves running counter to the gods and culture of our society.

How does this apply to us today? In what ways does your lifestyle reflect who God is?

_____

_____

In what ways might you be breaking the first commandment?

_____

_____

More Scriptures to Consider

1 Chronicles 16:29: "Ascribe to the Lord the glory due his name. Bring an offering and come before him; worship the Lord in the splendor of his holiness."

Psalm 95:6-7: "Come, let us bow down in worship, let us kneel before the Lord our Maker; for he is our God and we are the people of his pasture, the flock under his care."

2 Chronicles 29:30: "King Hezekiah and his officials ordered the Levites to praise the Lord with the words of David and of Asaph the seer. So they sang praises with gladness and bowed their heads and worshiped."

Day 4: What Does God Require of New Testament Worshipers?

As the New Testament opens, we find that things have changed. The Promised One has come; Light has entered the world. The One in whom all the fullness of the Godhead dwells has been fleshed out among us. Now Jesus Christ, the Messiah, has come. How is this going to affect worship? Is it going to change? It doesn't take long to discover that nothing has changed fundamentally. What worship meant in the past, as taught in Old Testament days, worship still means in the present.

The first reference to worship in the New Testament is recorded in Matthew 2:2, where the Magi sought the place where the "king of the Jews" had been born. Their purpose in searching for Him was to worship Him. The word used here is the Greek word *proskuneo*, meaning "to bow, crouch, stoop, or kneel," with the added picture of "kissing the hand" of the one you are worshiping. This is the word that is used later in Matthew 4, when Satan tempted our Lord in the wilderness by offering Him all the kingdoms of the world if He would but bow down and worship him. "All these things will I give You, if You fall down and worship me" (v. 9, NASB).

Satan knew that the issue of worship was at the heart of the battle between God and himself. He knew that if the Son of God could be persuaded to worship him the victory would be his. The battle would be over. Jesus' reply to Satan left no doubt, however, that Jesus, the Son of God, knew that Satan was trying to do what he had failed to accomplish in eternity past when he had tried to unseat God from His throne. Jesus said: "Away from me, Satan! For it is written, 'Worship the Lord your God, and serve him only'" (v. 10).

The word Jesus used here is the same word He used when He later spoke to the Samaritan woman about the Father seeking for those who would worship Him "in spirit and in truth." So we find that the heart attitude of worship has not changed from the Old Testament. It is the same as it was under the Old Covenant. But now, because the Lord Jesus is the fulfillment of the Old Covenant of the Law, New Covenant believers obey God's command to worship by worshiping through Christ, in Christ, and for Christ. Worship now is a response to the nature of God and His self-revelation through His Son. New Testament worship is a response to who God is in Christ.

Read the Scripture verses for today (Heb. 10:19-22). Now read it carefully, again and describe what makes the worship of all believers

Therefore, brothers, since we have confidence to enter the Most Holy Place by the blood of Jesus, by a new and living way opened for us through the curtain, that is, his body, and since we have a great priest over the house of God, let us draw near to God with a sincere heart in full assurance of faith, having our hearts sprinkled to cleanse us from a guilty conscience and having our bodies washed with pure water.

— Hebrews 10:19-22

How much more, then, will the blood of Christ, who through the eternal Spirit offered himself unblemished to God, cleanse our consciences from acts that lead to death, so that we may serve [worship] the living God!

— Hebrews 9:14

acceptable to God in a way that it could never have been accepted under the Old Covenant.

_____

_____

_____

_____

In the Old Testament the only access God's people had to the holy of holies, where God's presence dwelt and where the highest form of worship took place, was through the high priest. He was instructed by God to enter this most holy place once a year, on the Day of Atonement, with a blood sacrifice on behalf of the nation. But now in Hebrews 9:11-12,14 we read that: "When Christ came as high priest of the good things that are already here, he went through the greater and more perfect tabernacle that is not man-made, that is to say, not a part of this creation. He did not enter by means of the blood of goats and calves; but he entered the Most Holy Place once for all by his own blood, having obtained eternal redemption. . . . How much more, then, will the blood of Christ, who through the eternal Spirit offered himself unblemished to God, cleanse our consciences from acts that lead to death, so that we may serve [worship] the living God!"

These verses describe the confidence New Covenant believers have in approaching God in worship and prayer. We no longer have to go through an earthly high priest, nor do we have to make blood sacrifices anymore. The attitude of heart that God looks for has not changed, only the method. All blood-washed children of God are received into God's presence through the One who purchased them with His blood. There is no more man-made tabernacle on earth where God dwells. The tabernacle spoken of in this passage is the one in heaven. God's dwelling on earth is now "in" His people. Nor is there any longer a high priest on earth. Our Great High Priest dwells, and intercedes, in heaven on behalf of His people.

And there are no more blood sacrifices for sin to be offered because sin has been paid for in full. We are no longer separated from the presence of God by a curtain because the veil has been torn in two.

Read the poem in the sidebar. It describes what Christ has done for us. In two or three sentences, explain this in your own words.

_____

_____

_____

_____

What can we learn, and what application can we make to our own personal lives? What can we do to function better as the worshipers God created us to be? Go back and read the Scripture at the beginning of today's lesson (Heb. 10:19-22). In the context of what we have been studying today, what implications does it have for your life?

_____

_____

_____

_____

The severed veil, His body slain,
His blood upon the altar lain
Has given us the right to come
And bow before the heavenly throne.
Christ entered that Most Holy Place
And once for all the Savior placed
His own spilt blood and this sufficed—
There would be no more sacrifice.

We now can enter on our own,
We can ourselves approach the throne,
And kneel by His eternal grace
and talk to God face to face.
Clothed in the righteousness of Him
Whose blood has washed away our sin,
The earthly priesthood now has ceased,
And there remains but one High Priest.

HALLELUJAH! The debt's been paid,
The final payment has been made!

—Ron Owens "Paid in Full" © 1982 Ron & Patricia Owens

Jesus heard that they had thrown him out, and when he found him, he said, "Do you believe in the Son of Man?" "Who is he, sir?" the man asked. "Tell me so that I may believe in him." Jesus said, "You have now seen him; in fact, he is the one speaking with you." Then the man said, "Lord, I believe," and he worshiped him.

— John 9:35-38

Day 5: What Is the Relationship Between Worship and the New Birth?

You may have heard of Jesus' healing the blind man by putting mud on the man's eyes. Because this happened on the sabbath, the religious leaders investigated to see if a sin had been committed. After two interviews, they threw out the man that had been healed.

John 9:35-38 is what happened next. In fact, the main message in this ninth chapter of John is the spiritual healing of the blind man, not the physical healing. The greatest illness for anyone is to be spiritually blind. After all, what good is physical healing and a lot of excitement if that person will be lost eternally? if nothing of eternal value takes place?

In our day many people are more interested in physical needs than they are in spiritual needs. Healing meetings attract large crowds. Though God can and does heal us physically, that kind of healing is of no eternal worth unless there is spiritual healing.

But what does the story in John 9 have to do with worship? Actually this chapter has everything to do with worship because it deals with the role worship plays in conversion and the part conversion plays in the birthing of a worshiper.

There are four things to observe in this divine encounter. We will look at them and see how they apply to us and how they all led to this man's becoming a worshiper.

1. Though the man was physically healed, he was not yet a believer. His response to Jesus' question, "Do you believe in the Son of Man?" makes clear that this man had only been physically healed. "Who is He, Sir tell me so that I may believe in him," he replied (v. 36). From this we see that one can actually experience a miracle of healing from God and still be lost.

This man had had an unusual encounter. That morning when he had awakened he was blind. By that afternoon he could see perfectly. He had given testimony to the religious leaders that he believed Jesus was surely a prophet sent from God or else he could not have performed such a miracle. His question to them about their perhaps "also" being interested in becoming Jesus' disciples indicated that he already considered himself to be one.

In all probability the testimony of this man sounded as if he was a believer in Jesus. Yet he was still lost. It takes more than having some physical or emotional experience to become a new creation in Jesus Christ.

2. Revelation precedes salvation. Jesus must first reveal Himself to the person who is spiritually blind before that person can see the need for change (v. 37). Until the light is turned on, anyone who has lived in the dark all his life cannot see what he is like. We were all born into the pitch black condition of sin. Not until Jesus comes to us in our darkness can we see our need of a Savior.

This has always been true. When Jesus came to Saul, a Pharisee, and "revealed" Himself as the One he was persecuting, Saul made an about-face and would never look back. He became the Apostle Paul who would be the early church's greatest missionary, and who would ultimately lay down his life for his Lord.

When Jesus revealed who He was to Simon Peter, through the "great fish catch," Peter fell at the Lord's feet and confessed that he was a sinful man. Peter would end up laying down his life for his Lord (Luke 5).

When, through Philip, the Lord revealed who He was to the Ethiopian Eunuch, he became a believer (Acts 8:34-38). There is no salvation without a revelation of who Jesus is. When we say, "Lord, I believe," in the light of who we see Him to be, we become aware of our own lostness.

Seeing the Savior as our only hope of being delivered from eternal death, we respond as this healed blind man did. In humility and gratitude we confess Him as Lord and Savior, and we receive His gift of eternal life.

Read Acts 8:34-38. Can you recall the time, or the process, by which you were led to an understanding of who Jesus really is? Describe that time.

_____

_____

_____

If you cannot describe that time in your life, reread the Acts 8:34-38 passage again. Is Jesus revealing Himself to you? Explain.

_____

_____

The eunuch asked Philip, "Tell me, please, who is the prophet talking about, himself or someone else?" Then Philip began with that very passage of Scripture and told him the good news about Jesus. As they traveled along the road, they came to some water and the eunuch said, "Look, here is water. Why shouldn't I be baptized?" And he gave orders to stop the chariot. Then both Philip and the eunuch went down into the water and Philip baptized him.

— Acts 8:34-38

This is what the high and lofty One says—he who lives forever, whose name is holy: "I live in a high and holy place, but also with him who is contrite and lowly in spirit."

— Isaiah 57:15

3. *There is no redemption without an attitude of worship.* The moment the healed man realized that Jesus was the Messiah, he responded with the response of a humble, worshiping heart. Look carefully at what he said and did. "'Lord, I believe,' and he worshiped him" (John 9:38). The first word he spoke when he realized who Jesus was, was, "Lord." That word alone was an expression of worship. In saying "Lord," he was confessing the "lordship" of the one he was addressing. This was one who was worthy of worship. This was the one for whom the Jews had been praying and waiting for so long. This was the Messiah. "Lord, I believe!" said the man. "And he worshiped him."

This healed blind man demonstrated the kind of heart in which God takes up residence. God speaks of the humble of heart in Isaiah 57:15. "This is what the high and lofty One says—he who lives forever, whose name is holy: 'I live in a high and holy place, but also with him who is contrite and lowly in spirit.'" It was a heart that, upon realizing who was speaking to him, would fall to his knees, and worship. There is no salvation without this attitude of response to who Jesus is.

4. *There is no salvation without repentance.* Acts 3:19, KJV, says: "Repent . . . therefore, and be converted, that your sins may be blotted out." This man's response to the Savior revealed a repentant heart without which there is no new birth. A worshiping heart, the kind God is seeking, is a repentant heart. A person who says, "Lord," but has no plans to submit to the will of the One whom they are calling "Lord" is only making a confession of the lips, without believing in the heart. Romans 10:9 says: "If you confess with your mouth, 'Jesus is Lord,' and believe in your heart that God raised him from the dead, you will be saved."

This man demonstrated the kind of heart King David expressed in his psalm of repentance: "The sacrifices of God are a broken spirit; a broken and contrite heart, O God, you will not despise" (Ps. 51:17). A repentant, broken, contrite heart, is a heart that is ready to become a true worshiper. At the moment of new birth, the relationship with God that was broken at the Fall is again restored. At new birth the saved sinner becomes a worshiper.

Have you ever worshiped God? Relate a time when you know that you truly have worshiped God with a repentant, broken, and contrite, heart.

_____

_____

Why God Is So Central in Worship

The Ten Commandments were the basis of the Old Testament Law and the basis of God's standard of living for His people. This standard, set thousands of years ago, is as relevant today as it was when Moses carried those tablets down the mountain. The first four commands deal directly with our relationship with God and His requirements for worship. The final six deal with our relationship with God as we relate to our fellow man. The final six relate to worship since our obedience to them determines whether what we offer God in worship will be acceptable.

God's commandments reveal His character, who He is. We must know Him so we can obey Him and live. As we obey Him, God is glorified before a watching world in and through His people. The world will come to know what God is like and how they too can have life from Him, when they see Him made manifest through His people. This is God's eternal plan. God did not give us commandments to restrict us but to liberate us so we can live within the freedom He provides for us.

The reason God is so central in worship is because "the Lord is your life" (Deut. 30:20). Speaking with a word from God, Moses clearly declared to God's people: "This day I call heaven and earth as witnesses against you that I have set before you life and death, blessings and curses. Now choose life, so that you and your children may live and that you may love the Lord your God, listen to his voice, and hold fast to him. For the Lord is your life, and he will give you many years in the land he swore to give to your fathers, Abraham, Isaac and Jacob" (Deut. 30:19-20).

Jesus stated this same truth clearly as well: "Apart from me you can do nothing" (John 15:5), and, "The words I have spoken to you are spirit and they are life" (John 6:63).

Key Verse

One of the teachers . . . asked him, "Of all the commandments, which is the most important?" "The most important one," answered Jesus, "is this: 'Hear, O Israel, the Lord our God, the Lord is one. Love the Lord your God with all your heart and with all your soul and with all your mind and with all your strength.'"

— Mark 12:28-30

This Week's Lessons

1. What Does God Say About Himself?

2. How Does the Way We Live and Worship Glorify God?

3. Why Is God's Name So Important to Him?

4. What Is the Sabbath?

5. Is the Sabbath Still Relevant Today?

The measure in which we know God is the measure in which we will be able to worship Him. The way we get to know God is through the Scriptures, experienced in real life. In the Scriptures we have the revelation of God's nature and His ways. The truth of who He is, is affirmed and refined in experience.

Day 1: What Does God Say About Himself?

It is a transforming experience to worship God as He really is. God knew this when He gave His people the Ten Commandments. God made clear in the verse immediately preceding these commandments (Ex. 20:2) that He was: (1) the Lord; (2) their God; (3) who brought them out of the land of Egypt and out of bondage; and (4) therefore there would be absolutely no other God that they would ever worship.

Only God could have done for them what He had done. By His presence and power, His people were free. There was no other god who could do this. He impressed on them again and again, "I am God, and there is no other" (Isa. 45:22; 46:9). Therefore, to turn to anything else was to forsake Him. As His people, He alone would be their very life.

At Mt. Sinai He was making a covenant with His people, and He was declaring that He was the Lord God. Even as He had shown Himself to them as their Deliverer, in freeing them from Egyptian slavery, He would, from that point on, be revealing Himself to them, as a nation, in hundreds of different ways. Each one would be an expression of His character—who He is. In knowing Him they would know how to relate to Him and walk with Him. Especially would they know how to approach Him in worship.

The Hebrew word translated as "Lord" in Exodus 3:15 and 6:3 literally means "I Am" in Hebrew. Moses and the Israelites had learned firsthand that God controlled the weather, armies, the sea, life, and death, and that He could deliver His people. Think about the contrast between the God who can deliver and God known as I AM. If you, like the Israelites, had thought of God only in terms of what He could do specifically, how would your understanding be changed by knowing Him now as I AM?

_____

_____

_____

Each time God revealed Himself to His people, they learned a little more about how to approach Him. Let's look at several ways God revealed Himself, or pictured Himself, to His people in His Word and how such revelation related to their worship of Him. Remember, each time

God revealed Himself He urged them to be like Him, for they were His and would manifest Him to a watching world. Each time they accurately expressed Him to the world He would be glorified through them.

When believers give testimony to what God has done in their lives, they express God to the world. Give a brief testimony about the way in which God expressed Himself through you to another person.

_____

_____

_____

In Leviticus 11:44-45, God revealed to His people who He was. That revelation was to shape who they were, and how they were to live before Him and worship Him: "I am the Lord your God; consecrate yourselves and be holy, because I am holy . . . I am the Lord who brought you up out of Egypt to be your God; therefore be holy, because I am holy." (For further study, read Leviticus 19:2; 20:7, 26; 1 Peter 1:15-16.)

Worship, in His presence, brought His people face-to-face with Holy God. In worship they were constantly reminded of His holiness. And this holiness would always reveal their sin. This is still true in our own day. Our worship brings us face-to-face with Holy God, and He still says to His people, "Be holy, as I am holy!"

> "Consecrate yourselves and be holy, because I am the Lord your God."
> — Leviticus 20:7

> But just as he who called you is holy, so be holy in all you do; for it is written: "Be holy, because I am holy."
> — 1 Peter 1:15-16

Does the holiness of God affect the worship in your life, or your church? If not, why? If it does, how has God brought this about in your life and church?

_____

_____

_____

In worship God seeks to draw us to Himself, reveal our sin, and cleanse us of our sin. In lives transformed by His holiness, He then blesses His people with unlimited blessings and guides them in His ways, which always lead to fullness of life, peace, and joy. Jesus reinforced this connection between the nature of God, and His own personal love for His people, when He declared: "As the Father has loved me, so have I loved you. Now remain in my love. If you obey my command, you will remain in my love, just as I have obeyed my Father's commands and remain in his love. I have told you this so that my joy may be in you and that your joy may be complete" (John 15:9-11).

God is Love, and He commands His people to love as He has loved them (John 13:34-35). In worship we encounter Him and His love, as He guides us and we obey Him. Further, Jesus exemplified love from the Father to His disciples, and He said that as they loved one another, "by this all men will know that you are my disciples, if you love one another" (v. 35).

God is righteous in all His ways. Therefore, He urges His people to walk in righteousness in all their ways. We are to be "instruments of righteousness" to God (Rom. 6:13-20).

God is merciful, and we are to be merciful: "Love your enemies, do good to them, and lend to them without expecting to get anything back. Then your reward will be great, and you will be sons of the Most High, because he is kind to the ungrateful and wicked. Be merciful, just as your Father is merciful" (Luke 6:35-36).

Read Luke 6:32-36. This passage reveals a command that some believers may feel justified in ignoring. After reading the passage, who are people presuming to be the greater authority if they decide not to show kindness or mercy to someone? Explain.

_____

_____

_____

In worship the Holy Spirit helps us, usually through the Scriptures, come face-to-face with God. He reveals His nature and draws us to a decision about our own life as a child of God. Will I let God now transform me to be more like Him, or will I merely go through the motions of religious activity? Will I merely acknowledge Him, or will I be changed by Him? Every believer must make these decisions.

Let's now return to the Ten Commandments. The first four of these commandments help us respond to God in worship, and in life:

"You shall have no other gods before me" (Ex. 20:3) Since He is the

"If you love those who love you, what credit is that to you? Even 'sinners' love those who love them. And if you do good to those who are good to you, what credit is that to you? . . . Even 'sinners' lend to 'sinners,' expecting to be repaid in full. But love your enemies, do good to them, and lend to them without expecting to get anything back. Then your reward will be great, and you will be sons of the Most High, because he is kind to the ungrateful and wicked. Be merciful, just as your Father is merciful."

— Luke 6:32-36

only true God there is, to permit any other god to remain in our life is to deny and reject Him and to rob ourselves of any benefit from Him. Other gods are fatal to our relationship with God, and therefore endanger life itself for the Christian.

"You shall not make for yourself an idol in the form of anything in heaven above or on the earth beneath or in the waters below . . . for I, the Lord your God, am a jealous God" (Ex. 20:4-5). He is jealous for His name's sake, in our lives and homes. Any "image" is a substitute for God, and fatal for our lives.

"You shall not misuse the name of the Lord your God" (Ex. 20:7). Do not empty Him of His revealed nature. It is fatal to misread or misjudge God's nature by misusing His name. Don't live contrary to the full nature of God, as He has come to let you know Him. It is your life. In worship, everything that is true to His name must prevail. Nothing contrary to, or a substitute for, or a distortion of who He is, is permitted. God has transformed us to be like Him, and we bear His name. Therefore any misuse of His name that portrays Him in any other way than He is, is sin.

Exodus 20:7 says, "You shall not take the name of the Lord your God in vain" (NASB). With this in mind, how cautious should we be in using God's name in humor or, to endorsing or recommending political, business, or charitable causes? In answering, keep in mind that as believers, everything we do reflects on His name.

_____

_____

_____

_____

"Remember the sabbath day, to keep it holy" (Ex. 20:8, KJV). How we live out the Sabbath reveals what we believe about God. This commandment will be dealt with much more completely in days 4 and 5. It is enough to say, "The Sabbath is holy to the Lord" (Isa. 58:13-14).

The other six commandments deal with how, as holy children of God, we are to relate to others. As God is holy, all that is His, is holy. As we treat others, we are treating Him. Worship, therefore, requires that we be right with our brother in order to be right with God. Not to be right

Since He is the only true God there is, to permit any other god to remain in our life is to deny and reject Him and to rob ourselves of any benefit from Him. Other gods are fatal to our relationship with God, and therefore endanger life itself for the Christian.

with our brother is to forfeit the possibility of offering acceptable worship. Jesus said, "First go and be reconciled to your brother; then come and offer your gift" (Matt. 5:24). Reconciliation with your brother is prerequisite to an acceptable offering. God has reconciled us, therefore we are to be a reconciler to others. We cannot worship contrary to God's nature.

If we cannot worship contrary to God's nature, what are some possible barriers to your worship? What would it take to remove them?

_____

_____

_____

_____

"Therefore, if you are offering your gift at the altar and there remember that your brother has something against you, leave your gift there in front of the altar. First go and be reconciled to your brother; then come and offer your gift."

— Matthew 5:23-24

Day 2: How Does the Way We Live and Worship Glorify God?

As God's people, we have been given the privilege and responsibility of manifesting, or presenting, a correct image of God to the world. "Man's chief end is to glorify God and enjoy Him forever" (Westminster shorter catechism). One of the basic meanings of *glorify* is "to give a correct interpretation of something or someone." This is at the heart of our being "light and salt" in the world.

Jesus said, "Let your light so shine before men, that they may see your good works, *and glorify your Father in heaven*" (Matt. 5:16, NASB, our emphasis). Jesus had said to His disciples that He was "the light of the world" (John 8:12; 9:5). But because of the disciples' special relationship to Him, He also said to them, "You are the light of the world" (Matt. 5:14). Because He lived within them, they would manifest Him to their world. When they correctly and completely let Him live out His life in them and through them, the world would see Him through His disciples. In Jesus' prayer in the garden, He said to the Father, "I am glorified in them" (John 17:10, KJV). Just as Jesus could say, "He who has seen Me has seen the Father" (John 14:9, NASB), so He would indicate that when the world sees His disciples living out their relationship with Him, the world would "see Him."

So important was the disciples' relationship with Jesus and the Father that Jesus prayed to His Father, "That all of them may be one, Father, just as you are in me and I am in you. May they also be in us so *that the world may believe that you have sent me*" (John 17:21, our emphasis). The way we live and worship does redemptively, and eternally, affect much in the kingdom of God. If we live or "walk, even as he walked" (1 John 2:6), the world will know Him and know how to respond to Him in a saving way. However, if we fail to live as He is in us, the world will not know Him through us and may be eternally lost.

This is why it is so vital that God's people truly worship as God designed worship. For in His presence, in a full encounter with Him, He carefully and faithfully reveals anything in us that is not like Him. Knowing how our lives affect the kind of encounter with God others will have through us, we must immediately repent when sin is revealed in us and return to a holy relationship with Him. Paul was deeply convinced that this was true, as he said, "I have been crucified with Christ and I no longer live, but Christ lives in me. The life I live in the body, I live by faith in the Son of God, who loved me and gave himself for me. I do not set aside the grace of God" (Gal. 2:20-21).

The way we live and worship does redemptively, and eternally, affect much in the kingdom of God. If we live or "walk, even as he walked" (1 John 2:6), the world will know Him and know how to respond to Him in a saving way. However, if we fail to live as He is in us, the world will not know Him through us and may be eternally lost.

"I have been crucified with Christ and I no longer live, but Christ lives in me. The life I live in the body, I live by faith in the Son of God, who loved me and gave himself for me. I do not set aside the grace of God."

— Galatians 2:20-21

Read Galatians 2:20-21 again. How important is it that we live and walk just as Jesus lived and walked? Why?

_____

_____

_____

_____

Scriptures help us know how we can glorify God in the way we live and the way we worship. In times of great revival, when God's people powerfully worshiped God, encountering Him and repenting and returning fully to Him, hundreds, even tens of thousands of lost people came to saving faith in Christ. This was so in the great moving of God in Wales in 1904–05, and in Northern Ireland in 1859. As God's people worshiped, and out of worship lived transformed lives before their watching world, multitudes came under conviction concerning their relationship to a Holy God and were saved.

Jesus said to the Father, "I glorified Thee on the earth" (John 17:4, NASB). He was saying that He had lived in such harmony with God that there was never a time or a moment when God could not fully be revealed through Him. Jesus lived in such a way that those who met Him met the Father. This was true when Peter first met Jesus in this way. In Luke 5, Jesus taught, then challenged Peter to go out and let down his nets for a catch. The catch was so overwhelming that Peter's response was immediate: "Go away from me, Lord; I am a sinful man!" (v. 8). Jesus invited Peter to join Him for the rest of his life. And he did, not only himself being transformed but being used of God to lead many others to be transformed by their own encounter with Him.

The way we live and worship first transforms us; then through us other lives are transformed as well. Others ought to be convinced of a number of things about God as they watch us worship. They should see that . . .

1. God is holy.
2. God hates sin.
3. God redeems the sinner.
4. God grants fullness of life to His people.
5. God is on mission to redeem our world.
6. God requires obedience and blesses obedience.

7. God grants to His people great mercy and grace.
8. God grants to His people great power and boldness.

Review this list of God's characteristics that worship should reflect. Is this the normal worship experience in your own life? in your church, week after week? Are others trembling before Holy God, just watching you worship? Does the entire community of your congregation sense the awesome presence of God when you worship? Describe what you are thinking.

_____

_____

_____

_____

When the early church worshiped, the entire city of Jerusalem trembled (Acts 2–4). True worship transforms the worshiper and affects the world. When this happens, God is greatly glorified (revealed before a watching world). I remember a moment on a university campus when we were worshiping God. The auditorium was full. God was present as His Word was proclaimed. Suddenly two young men ran forward, deeply convicted of their sin. They asked to share. As they did, hundreds of other students came under great conviction and began to cry out to God, too.

This lasted all night and for days to come. Other places heard what God had done and asked for someone to share on their campus. Revival broke out on a seminary campus, then on more than one hundred other campuses over the months to come. It all began in a moment of true worship—just like it has been told us in the Scriptures (i.e., 2 Chron. 7:14).

> "If my people, who are called by my name, will humble themselves and pray and seek my face and turn from their wicked ways, then will I hear from heaven and will forgive their sin and will heal their land."
> — 2 Chronicles 7:14

Would you please stop and pray that God will transform your life when you worship so that He can be revealed as He really is to others for their sake? If you will, when you have finished praying, write "Amen!" to mark your commitment to be transformed in worship.

_____

_____

God never acts or functions contrary to His nature. He would have to cease to be God to do so.

Day 3: Why Is God's Name So Important to Him?

God's name is His essential nature. His name is who God is. And God never acts or functions contrary to His nature. He would have to cease to be God to do so. If we get His name wrong (even 1 percent off), it is no longer God we worship.

Calling Him "Lord!" does not mean He is Lord in us. As a matter of fact, to call Him Lord and then live or act contrary to His name is to blaspheme His name. This would be to "take His name in vain" and thus break the Third Commandment.

When God's people do not live out through their lives, a true reflection of God's character (name), it causes unbelievers to stumble in their understanding of God—and even for them to blaspheme His name. When David sinned against God by committing adultery with Bathsheba and causing the death of her husband, Uriah, God announced to David through the prophet Nathan, that he had "given great occasion to the enemies of the Lord to blaspheme" (2 Sam. 12:14, KJV). This was incredibly serious with God. David had put a spiritual stumbling block in the way of those God would redeem. God had to judge David, to restore His name, to restore David.

God said that His people had profaned "my holy name . . . among the nations" (Ezek. 36:21). Then God announced, in great seriousness, "I will show the holiness of my great name, which has been profaned among the nations, the name you have profaned among them. Then the nations will know that I am the Lord, declares the Sovereign Lord, when I show myself holy through you before their eyes" (Ezek. 36:23). In order to restore His name in the eyes of the nations, He would place His people in 70 years of bondage in Babylon.

God then adds, "This is what the Sovereign Lord says: It is not for your sake, O house of Israel, that I am going to do these things, but for the sake of my holy name, which you have profaned among the nations where you have gone" (Ezek. 36:22).

To know Him, as He is, is our very life, both in time and in eternity. This is why His name is so important to Him. Therefore, our worship must be consistent with His name, or His people will stray from Him and ultimately be of no use to Him to redeem a lost world. In private or in corporate worship, the first element in our prayer must be: "Our Father in heaven, hallowed be your name, your kingdom come, your will be done on earth as it is in heaven" (Matt. 6:9-10). Did you notice the connected sequence in Jesus' model prayer: (1) His name must be kept holy. (2) When this is true, then His kingdom will come on earth, and His will will be done. (3) And His will be the "glory forever."

Based on Matthew 6:9-10, is a congregation taking God's name in vain when they fail to join Him in redeeming a lost world? Explain.

_____

_____

_____

> "This, then, is how you should pray: 'Our Father in heaven, hallowed be your name, your kingdom come, your will be done on earth as it is in heaven.'"
>
> Matthew 6:9-10

Everything in our life and worship depends on His name being holy in us. That is, His character and nature will not be violated, or changed, or altered, by the way we speak, or behave, or act. Think of the following ways in which His name is so vital:

- We are called by His name (2 Chron. 7:14).
- We gather in His name (Matt. 18:20).
- We pray in His name (John 14:13-14).
- We live by faith in His name (Acts 3:16).
- We proclaim His name (Ex. 9:16).
- We are baptized in His name (Matt. 28:19).
- We put our hope in His name (Matt. 12:21).

Peter stated clearly, "Salvation is found in no one else, for there is no other name under heaven given to men by which we must be saved" (Acts 4:12). When Peter gathered with Cornelius and his family in worship, he shared about Jesus, saying, "All the prophets testify about him that everyone who believes in him receives forgiveness of sins through his name" (Acts 10:43).

This is why His name is so important to Him. The eternal redemption of the world rests upon it. When we worship, we must not violate anything about His name. For the very lives of those who are present rest on His name. In Revelation 22:1-5, His name is mentioned for the last time in Scripture, and it has to do with His name being written on our foreheads. First John 3:2 says that "we shall be like him, for we shall see him as he is."

We close this day's study with an urgent call from Paul, the apostle, "Whatever you do, whether in word or deed, do it all in the name of the Lord Jesus, giving thanks to God the Father through him" (Col. 3:17).

Day 4: What Is the Sabbath?

> "Remember the Sabbath day by keeping it holy. Six days you shall labor and do all your work, but the seventh day is a Sabbath to the Lord your God. On it you shall not do any work, neither you, nor your son or daughter, nor your manservant or maidservant nor your animals, nor the alien within your gates."
>
> — Exodus 20:8-10

God is always concerned that His people be clearly identified as being different, set apart from the world. They are a covenant people—chosen, called, and separated from all other peoples. They are holy, sanctified by God, and separated to God by His sovereign choice. One of the established differences was to be the Sabbath!

In the act of creation, God established a clear way for His creation to know Him as Creator and Lord. He did this by creating a seventh day and sanctifying it: "God blessed the seventh day and made it holy, because on it he rested from all the work of creating that he had done" (Gen. 2:3). For all time the seventh day belonged to God and was to be lived out in recognition that He is Lord of all. How people, especially His people, lived out the Sabbath according to God's commands would always stand as a witness to God and to man that He is Lord! God incorporated the Sabbath into the marching orders of His newly created people, Israel. The Fourth Commandment stated: "Remember the Sabbath day by keeping it holy. Six days you shall labor and do all your work, but the seventh day is a Sabbath to the Lord your God. . . . The Lord blessed the Sabbath day and made it holy" (Ex. 20:8-11).

But God added two other reasons He set apart and sanctified the Sabbath. First, it would forever be a "sign" between God and His chosen people, that He had redeemed them and sanctified them for Himself forever.

> "Say to the Israelites, 'You must observe my Sabbaths. This will be a sign between me and you for the generations to come, so you may know that I am the Lord, who makes you holy. . . . It is holy to you. . . . It will be a sign between me and the Israelites forever.'"
>
> — Exodus 31:13-14,17

Read the excerpt from Exodus 31:13-17. List one way you demonstrate, at least once a week, the covenant between you and God.

_____

_____

_____

Describe the kind of impact you believe God could have on your life if you set aside the Sabbath as holy, as a time when He brought *you* out of darkness and into the light.

_____

_____

Second, God added another reminder to His people of how special they were to Him: "Observe the Sabbath day by keeping it holy. . . . Remember that you were slaves in Egypt and that the Lord your God brought you out of there with a mighty hand and an outstretched arm. Therefore the Lord your God has commanded you to observe the Sabbath day" (Deut. 5:12-15).

This was God's instruction through Moses' 40 plus years after Mount Sinai, in the second giving of the law, just before they entered the promised land. Thus, the Sabbath has a threefold significance for God's people:

1. To acknowledge that He alone is Lord.
2. To acknowledge that He is their Creator.
3. To acknowledge that He is their Redeemer and Sanctifier, their God.

Therefore, how the people of God kept the Sabbath said a lot about God. It was a major expression of worship. When they did not keep the Sabbath, their worship was no longer acceptable: "Be careful . . . on the Sabbath day. . . . Do not . . . do any work . . . , but keep the Sabbath day holy, as I commanded your forefathers. Yet they did not listen or pay attention; they were stiff-necked and would not listen or respond to discipline. . . . If you do not obey me to keep the Sabbath day holy, . . . then I will kindle an unquenchable fire in the gates of Jerusalem that will consume her fortresses" (Jer. 17:21-23,27).

God said He gave the Sabbath "as a sign between us, so they would know that I the Lord made them holy" (Ezek. 20:12).

Then God dealt radically with His people when they rebelled against Him in not keeping the Sabbath, and He did it "for the sake of my name I did what would keep it from being profaned in the eyes of the nations in whose sight I had brought them out" (Ezek. 20:14).

Review the threefold significance for God's people in keeping the Sabbath. How would your worship change if you regularly acknowledged God as Lord, Creator, and Redeemer and Sanctifier? What steps could you take to make this acknowledgment part of your worship?

_____

_____

_____

_____

"Therefore the Lord, the the God of Israel, declares: 'I promised that your house and your father's house would minister before me forever.' But now the Lord declares: 'Far be it from me! Those who honor me I will honor, but those who despise me will be disdained.'"

— 1 Samuel 2:30

Finally, in Isaiah 58:13-14, God guided them in the proper purpose and use for the Sabbath as a day of pure worship to God: "'If you keep your feet from breaking the Sabbath and from doing as you please on my holy day, if you call the Sabbath a delight and the Lord's holy day honorable, and if you honor it by not going your own way and not doing as you please or speaking idle words, then you will find your joy in the Lord, and I will cause you to ride on the heights of the land and to feast on the inheritance of your father Jacob.' The mouth of the Lord has spoken."

Look back over this day's section. Reflect on the content and answer this question: How do you worship and honor God by observing the Sabbath?

_____

_____

_____

_____

Day 5: Is the Sabbath Still Relevant Today?

Long before the Law—in creation—God sanctified the Sabbath for Himself. He gave it to His people, for them to worship Him and acknowledge that He is their God who sanctified them. As they did, it would always be a strong and clear witness to the unbelieving world around them.

The key was not the "letter of the law" that it had to be Saturday. God's command was simply, "Six days you shall labor and do all your work, but the seventh day is a Sabbath to the Lord your God" (Ex. 20:9-10; Deut. 5:13-14).

It is obvious that the early church worked six days and rested on what was to them God's most significant day—Sunday, the day of resurrection, when the "new creation" was completed! They called it "the Lord's Day" (Rev. 1:10). From the first century until today, the "first day of the week" has been the Christians' Sabbath to the Lord (Acts 20:7; 1 Cor. 16:2).

We face a similar threat to the Lord's Day, as Israel did, and it cost them their very life. When we say, as they did, "We want to be like the nations, like the peoples of the world, who serve wood and stone" (Ezek. 20:32), God described their actions this way: "They rejected my laws and did not follow my decrees and desecrated my Sabbaths. For their hearts were devoted to their idols" (Ezek. 20:16).

They wanted to please the unbelieving world around them. They wanted to be like the Gentiles. Some may have argued that by compromising they could win over the Gentiles to worship their God. History bears witness: This never works! The world draws Christians into their world, and the world despises believers for their compromise. If God does not mean that much in our hearts, why serve our God?

One of the idols in our world that God's people today have adopted into their hearts and therefore into their lives, and in so doing profane God's Sabbath, is sports. It is one of the biggest idols in our day. The world used to avoid sports on Sunday because of our Christian witness. Not any more. The Christian not only never complains about this, but too many Christians have actually joined the world. We let our children play on teams that play on Sunday, refusing to believe God will honor those who honor Him (1 Sam. 2:30).

We "worship" sports on Sunday. At first we gave in only if the sporting event was played on Sunday afternoon. But then the world began to add Sunday morning sports to its schedule, and many of God's people not only let their children profane the Sabbath but even encouraged

One of the idols in our world that God's people today have adopted into their hearts and therefore into their lives, and in so doing profane God's Sabbath, is sports. It is one of the biggest idols in our day.

them—and joined them. But beware! The cost is too high in our relationship to God. He is not mocked. Whatever we sow we reap. If we sow to the flesh and the world, we will reap corruption, and it will come out in our children and in their relationship to God. Parents and spiritual leaders cannot compromise (with human reasoning and not obeying God's Word) without paying a high price with God. An entire church that "tips their hat" to God on Sunday and uses the rest of the day for self-pleasure—no matter how we reason it (and we've heard most of the excuses, none based on Scripture)—is headed for spiritual disaster. God will withdraw His presence and power and blessing, even bringing judgment. The Sabbath is too serious with God not to pay strict attention to how we live it out before our watching world.

Read 1 Samuel 2:30. In what ways can you see that God is being dishonored by neglect of the sabbath? What could you do to honor Him more?

_____

_____

_____

_____

Jesus both warned and condemned those who in their outward activity seemed to be in obedience to God, but their hearts were far from Him: "These people honor me with their lips, but their hearts are far from me. They worship me in vain; their teachings are but rules taught by men" (Matt. 15:8-9).

Human reasoning, even if endorsed by church leaders, can never be a substitute for the commands of God. They will "worship in vain" if they try to do this.

Look at the commands of God, the standards and reasoning of God concerning the Sabbath. Carefully examine (because God does) how you are keeping this Fourth Commandment, given at creation and stated again so clearly in the Ten Commandments. If you are guilty of breaking this commandment, return to God quickly, for this is an essential aspect of true worship.

Read again the Fourth Commandment in Exodus 20:8-11. Do you find this verse somewhat troubling? In what ways do you and your congregation honor your covenant with God in worship and Sabbath activities?

_____

_____

_____

_____

You may want to look further at:

___ Use of TV, etc. as a substitute for Scripture and prayer at home on the Lord's Day.

___ Our eating in restaurants, instead of preparing ahead and eating in our homes.

___ What we read on Sunday.

___ The many "church meetings" we schedule on Sunday.

___ When we last spoke on the subject of the Sabbath in church, in Sunday School, or to our children at home.

___ See whether personally, as a church, or as a nation we may already be under the judgment of God for profaning His Sabbath before a watching world.

"Remember the Sabbath day by keeping it holy. Six days you shall labor and do all your work, but the seventh day is a Sabbath to the Lord your God. On it you shall not do any work, neither you, nor your son or daughter, nor your manservant or maidservant, nor your animals, nor the alien within your gates. For in six days the Lord made the heavens and the earth, the sea, and all that is in them, but he rested on the seventh day. Therefore the Lord blessed the Sabbath day and made it holy."

— Exodus 20:8-11

What Is God's Standard for Acceptable Worship?

The only standard that has remained unchanged throughout history is the standard of God's Word. In it God has revealed who He is and how His creation is to relate to Him. When God speaks, that's it. There is no discussion. In His Word we find His standard for worship, and it is as unchanging as God is. Just as God is the same yesterday, today, and forever, so are His standards for worship. Though man in His sinful thinking may shape for himself a god that fits his personal standards, this does not change the only standard against which all of God's children are judged.

Key Verse

I urge you, brothers, in view of God's mercy, to offer your bodies as living sacrifices, holy and pleasing to God—this is your spiritual act of worship.

— Romans 12:1

This Week's Lessons

1. Why Does God Require a Sacrifice?

2. What Kind of Sacrifice Does God Want Now?

3. When Does the Worshiper Become the Offering?

3. Are You a Getter or a Giver?

5. Are You Accepted or Rejected?

I am not worshiping God because of what He will do for me, but because of what He is to me. When worship becomes pragmatic, it ceases to be worship. R. G. Letourneau used to say, "If you give because it pays, it won't pay." The principle applies to worship; if you worship because it pays, it won't pay. Our motive must be to please God and glorify Him alone.

— Warren Wiersbe

Then the Lord said to Cain, "Why are you angry? Why is your face downcast? If you do what is right, will you not be accepted? But if you do not do what is right, sin is crouching at your door; it desires to have you, but you must master it."

— Genesis 4:6-7

Day 1: Why Does God Require a Sacrifice?

To find an answer to this question, we must go back to the first time a sacrifice was made. You recall how the relationship that God had had with Adam and Eve in the garden of Eden had been broken when they chose to disobey Him. Death had now entered the world. Things would never be the same again. But God did not give up on them. Though He could no longer fellowship with them as He had, His love for His creation did not change. In fact, His provision for restoring the broken relationship had already been made in eternity past, and that provision was the actual sacrifice of His own Son (1 Pet. 1:18-20). His Son had to die. But why such a drastic measure? Couldn't the restoring of the relationship been accomplished another way?

There is no way for us to understand how evil sin is in God's eyes. No human language can express how revolting it is to Him. It is the antithesis, the extreme opposite, of all He is and represents. There can be no compromise. God's condemnation of sin was so great that the only way it could be atoned for was through the death of someone or something. A sin offering, or sacrifice, would have to be made. Throughout the Old Testament we read God's instructions about the sin offering in which the life of an animal is taken for a temporary payment for sin. Sin offerings are mentioned no less than 120 times in Scripture. These, of course, were all foreshadowings of Calvary.

The first blood shed on earth came as a result of sin, when animals were slain in order to use their skins to cover the nakedness of Adam and Eve (Gen. 3:21). But the first actual recorded blood sacrifice took place some years later when Abel offered his sacrifice of one of the first-born from his flock. This offering was accepted by God, and thus the beginning of the bloodstream of redemption was established that continued until the death of our Messiah. Cain's offering was rejected by God because he, himself, was unacceptable. When Cain got angry, God said to him, "If you do what is right, will you not be accepted? But if you do not do what is right, sin is crouching at your door" (Gen. 4:7).

Read Genesis 4:6-7. Based on what these verses say, what makes our offerings and worship acceptable or unacceptable to God?

_____

_____

_____

Let's now look at the highlight points in this progression of re-demption, the history of the sin sacrifice.

It began with a lamb for a man. "Abel brought fat portions from some of the firstborn of his flock. The Lord looked with favor on Abel and his offering" (Gen. 4:4). That day the blood of one lamb was suf-ficient for the sins of one man.

At the Passover in Egypt it became a lamb for a family. "On the tenth day of this month each man is to take a lamb for his family, one for each household. . . . The animals you choose must be year-old males without defect" (Ex. 12:3,5).

This was the institution of the Passover, just prior to God's deliver-ing of His people from Egyptian bondage. God was about to send one final plague to Egypt in which the life of the firstborn of every family would be taken, except for those who would take the blood of a lamb and sprinkle it on the sides and above the door to their homes. God said, through Moses, that when He passed by that night He would spare every family where the blood had been applied to the doors of their dwelling places (Ex. 12:23). That night the blood of one lamb was suf-ficient for the protection of an entire family from God's wrath.

Then in Leviticus, as God continues to reveal further dimensions of the sin offering or sacrifice, it becomes a lamb for a nation. "This shall be an everlasting statute unto you, to make an atonement for the chil-dren of Israel for all their sins once a year" (Lev. 16:34, KJV).

Once a year for the sins of a nation? Do you see where it is head-ing? A lamb for a man, Abel. A lamb for a family at the Passover in Egypt. A lamb for a nation on the Day of Atonement.

Now, as the bloodstream of redemption reaches its climax, the sin offering, the sacrifice, becomes the Lamb for a world. When John the Baptist cried out: "Behold, the Lamb of God who takes away the sin of the world!" (John 1:29, NASB), he was not making an idle, casual state-ment. It was not coincidental that he used the words, "Lamb of God," for the Lamb of Atonement, the true Passover Lamb, was in their midst. Nor was it coincidental three years later, near the end of His ministry, that Jesus chose the Passover celebration, the Feast of Unleavened Bread, to picture to His disciples what was going to happen to Him, even as they ate the last supper together.

When Jesus hung on the cross just a few days later, a lamb was being slain—not just for a man, woman, boy, or girl; not just for families or nations; but finally a Lamb for a world. "God so loved the world, that he gave his only begotten Son" (John 3:16, KJV). That is a world that includes every one, who by faith, believes and receives God's gift of

When Jesus hung on the cross just a few days later, a lamb was being slain— not just for a man, woman, boy, or girl; not just for families or nations; but finally a Lamb for a world.

eternal life. This is the great news of the gospel. The perfect Lamb of God, "Christ, a lamb without blemish or defect" (1 Pet. 1:19), has paid the sacrifice God accepts for eternity in our behalf. No more sacrifice to atone for sin will ever be required or accepted.

No other lamb was found in all God's heaven,
　　to satisfy the awesome debt of sin,
Except one lamb, His only Son begotten;
　　God's just requirements all were met in Him.

—Ron & Patricia Owens © 1986

Review the "Progression of Redemption." As you reflect back on how God prepared His people across the centuries to receive the sacrifice of Jesus, express in your own words how the Lamb slain for the world also satisfies the necessary sacrifice for you, an individual. Share your understanding with at least one other person.

_____

_____

_____

_____

The Progression of Redemption

A lamb for a man (Gen. 4:4)

A lamb for a family (Ex. 12:3-5)

A lamb for a nation (Lev. 16:34)

The Lamb for the world (John 1:29)

Day 2: What Kind of Sacrifice Does God Want Now?

It is necessary for us to understand a fundamental difference between all the sin sacrifices that were made throughout the Old Testament and the final, complete sin sacrifice that was made by our Lord. The difference is this. Whereas the sin sacrifices of the Old Testament were animals that did not know what was happening and had already been slain before they were placed on the altar, our Lord knew what was happening, and His was a living sacrifice. He was alive on the altar of the cross.

Now, since His live and final sacrifice for sin has been made, the sacrifices that God is looking for from us are living sacrifices. During these next two days we are going to look at what this means and how it relates to our own personal and corporate worship as we, living sacrifices, become more and more transformed into the image of the One through whom we offer our worship.

Though our Scripture verse for today is 1 Peter 2:5, we need to read verses 1-11 in order to understand what Peter is talking about in verse 5.

In the latter part of chapter 1, Peter stresses the importance of God's Word and how it will abide forever. In week 1 we discussed the centrality of God's Word in worship—reading it and preaching it. Peter then ties the Word of God to what follows in chapter 2 with a "therefore." And the "therefore" addresses the need of heart and soul preparation for worship.

At the beginning of 1 Peter 2, Peter presents to the believers steps they need to take in order that they may offer "spiritual sacrifices acceptable to God" (1 Pet. 2:5). He makes this charge to them on the basis of their having been born again (1 Pet. 1:23) and on the assumption that they have also discovered the joy of fellowship with their Lord. "Now that you have tasted that the Lord is good." Peter makes plain to them that they need to lay aside "all malice and all deceit, hypocrisy, envy, and slander of every kind" (1 Pet. 2:1). Why? Because they were to live in continual fellowship with the Lord, the One "chosen by God and precious" (1 Pet. 2:4), and because they also had counted Him to be the most precious to their own lives. The basis of making "spiritual sacrifices" is always because of God's supreme "worthship" to our own lives. We will want to know the preparation and adjustments we need to make in our hearts in order to have unhindered access to His presence.

Read 1 Peter 2:1-5. In what ways are believers, like "living stones," to offer up spiritual sacrifices?" Put this in your own words, in terms that

> You also, like living stones, are being built into a spiritual house to be a holy priesthood, offering spiritual sacrifices acceptable to God through Jesus Christ.
>
> — 1 Peter 2:5

relate to how you have done this in your own life or have observed it in the lives of other believers.

_____

_____

_____

The sacrifice that God is looking for is one that is offered by clean hands and a pure heart.

David asks the question in Psalm 24:3, "Who may ascend the hill of the Lord? Who may stand in his holy place?" He then answers his own question: "He who has clean hands and a pure heart, who does not lift up his soul to an idol or swear by what is false" (v. 4). He goes on to say that this is the one who will receive the blessing of the Lord.

What kind of sacrifice is God seeking? A sacrifice that has been prepared. God gave detailed instructions to the priests under the Old Covenant regarding the preparation of the animals that would be used for sacrifice. Much care had to be taken to follow these instructions less the offering be unacceptable to God (Lev. 1).

Peter begins chapter 2 with a brief list of some of those things that would disqualify us from ascending the hill of the Lord to worship. He says: "Rid yourselves of all malice and all deceit, hypocrisy, envy, and slander of every kind" (v. 1). This is fundamental to true worship. How many today, when they attend the worship service, give little if any thought to checking their hearts to see if they have "clean hands." Too many give the impression that they believe God is delighted that they are even willing to pay Him a visit, no matter what spiritual shape their lives may be in. The sacrifice that God is looking for is one that is offered by clean hands and a pure heart.

What spiritual preparation do you make before you get to the worship service? Do you take seriously the required preparation God outlines in His Word?

_____

_____

_____

_____

Read Psalm 15. Read all five verses of this psalm and place your life against what God is saying here. What do you note about the comparison?

_____

_____

_____

The next thing Peter addresses is the focus of worship. In no uncertain terms he tells us what we have already stressed on day 2 of week 1, that under the New Covenant worship is through Christ, in Christ, and for Christ. He says we are to "come to him, the living Stone—rejected by men but chosen by God and precious to him" (v. 4). So what kind of sacrifice is God seeking? A sacrifice that is Christ centered and Christ honoring.

He is the One who motivates us to worship. "God made him who had no sin to be sin for us, so that in him we might become the righteousness of God" (2 Cor. 5:21). What greater motivation to worship could there be than this? He has delivered us out of sin that we might become the worshipers we were created to be.

We worship because of our Savior, who, though rejected by the world, is "precious" to us (1 Pet. 2:7). He has become the chief cornerstone (vv. 6-8). Upon Him is built everything that ever will be built that is of any lasting value, and upon Him is being built a spiritual house in which we, God's chosen, are living stones.

What kind of sacrifice does God want? The corporate sacrifice of living stones that make up a household of faith. "You also, like living stones, are being built into a spiritual house to be a holy priesthood, offering spiritual sacrifices acceptable to God through Jesus Christ" (1 Pet. 2:5).

This verse is one of the strongest statements in the Bible regarding the importance of the "gathering," the assembling of ourselves together for worship and fellowship. A better translation of this passage, one that is closer to the original language is, "as living stones, build yourselves up." It is something that we are constantly to be working on so that the corporate sacrifices we make will be pleasing to God. We are part of a household of faith. We don't attend church to "do our own thing," but to be a part of the whole. Some people have the attitude that they can do as they please, and if someone doesn't like it, too bad. "Don't tell

Who may dwell in your sanctuary? Who may live on your holy hill? He whose walk is blameless and who does what is righteous, who speaks the truth from his heart and has no slander on his tongue, who does his neighbor no wrong and casts no slur on his fellowman, who despises a vile man but honors those who fear the Lord, who keeps his oath even when it hurts, who lends his money without usury and does not accept a bribe against the innocent. He who does these things will never be shaken.

— Psalm 15

It is true that we stand before God as individuals and will be accountable to God for our own deeds, but when we gather for corporate worship, individual worshipers are suddenly seen as one body in Christ.

me what I can or cannot do." Such an attitude is foreign to what God wants when we gather to worship.

It is true that we stand before God as individuals and will be accountable to God for our own deeds, but when we gather for corporate worship, individual worshipers are suddenly seen as one body in Christ. Paul explained that "in Christ we who are many form one body, and each member belongs to all the others" (Rom. 12:5). Though we are individually, living stones, we are actually stones of a "living" entity, the church. Ephesians 2:19-22 talks about our being built together for a habitation of the Holy Spirit.

So we see that the kind of sacrifice God is seeking is a sacrifice that . . .

- Has been prepared.
- Is Christ centered.
- Is the corporate sacrifice of "living stones."

List three actions that would help you to be a sacrifice that is prepared and Christ centered and to function as a "living stone."

1. _____

2. _____

3. _____

Day 3: When Does the Worshiper Become the Offering?

Since the final sacrifice for sin was made through the death of our Savior on the cross, the offering God now looks for is a "living sacrifice" (Rom. 12:1-2). Do you realize that this means that you, yourselves, who are the worshipers, are now also the worship offering? When we approach God with our worship sacrifice, it is our own selves, our "body" that He is waiting for us to place on the altar. That is what God is seeking. Our singing, our praying, our teaching or preaching—no matter how excellent these may sound to human ears—do not impress God until He sees you and me on the worship altar.

We all want to give God what He desires. None of us want to fall short of what His intentions are for us. That is why it is so vital that we understand what it is He is looking for when it comes to offering Him worship. He is the object and subject of all true worship, and we find in the Scripture to be studied today that at the heart of New Testament worship is the offering of ourselves to God. The apostle Paul urges, beseeches, the believers in the church at Rome to surrender themselves, their bodies, to God.

Paul implies in his opening words in chapter 12, that the very presenting of our lives as living sacrifices is only possible because of God's mercy. You might say that there is an obligation to do so because of what God has done for us.

We who were doomed to die, we who were shackled by the chains of sin, we who were without any hope at all were set free from sin's bondage, and it was all because of God's mercy and love. Some of you will remember the old hymn that used to be sung a lot. The refrain goes like this:

> Mercy there was great, and grace was free;
> Pardon there was multiplied to me;
> There my burdened soul found liberty
> At Calvary.
> —William R. Newell

A hymn that was written during one of the Welsh revivals expresses God's love and mercy so beautifully. The last two lines say:

Grace and love like mighty rivers poured unending from above—
God's own peace and perfect justice kissed a guilty world with love.

How many of us would love a guilty world enough to reach out to

Therefore, I urge you, brothers, in view of God's mercy, to offer your bodies as living sacrifices, holy and pleasing to God—this is your spiritual act of worship. Do not conform any longer to the pattern of this world, but be transformed by the renewing of your mind. Then you will be able to test and approve what God's will is—his good, pleasing and perfect will.
— Romans 12:1-2

that world in this way? Who has given us an example of blessing law-breakers with grace and love?

_____

Aren't we commanded to be like Him?

_____

It was your world, it was my world, that God kissed with His love and mercy, so how can we do less in return than to surrender ourselves to Him, than to place our bodies on the altar and share His love and mercy with all others? And in Paul's admonition to us, relating to the worshiper's becoming the worship offering, he stresses five things:

1. The sacrifice we make will be a complete one. In his speaking about the presenting of our bodies, we have the picture of our bringing an offering or the presenting of ourselves as a gift to God. The apostle Paul is talking about our entire being, everything we are. God is not interested in partial sacrifices. Partial sacrifices are fine with the world, however. The world doesn't mind a Christian going to church on Sunday as long as that same Christian doesn't stand for righteousness in the marketplace, as long as he or she doesn't make waves during the week. They don't mind network television showing national leaders going to church with Bibles tucked under their arms just as long as they don't publically take a stand for what the Bible teaches. The world will go along with partial sacrifices, but God only accepts complete ones.

In the Old Testament the animals that were used for sacrifice were to be the best of the flock. The people were never to offer sick or injured animals (Lev. 3:1). If anything but the best was offered, the sacrifice was rejected. Has it changed in our day? Is God now satisfied with our offering Him a sacrifice that doesn't cost us anything?

The sacrifice God is looking for is a complete one, everything we are—a sacrifice that costs and counts. When we bring our worship offerings to God, let us bring complete offerings, the best we have and all we are.

2. The sacrifice we make will be a living one. As we said earlier, in Old Testament days the animals to be sacrificed were already dead when they were placed on the altar. The animals did not know what was happening, and they did not have a choice. When the Lamb of God became the sacrifice, however, His was a living, voluntary sacrifice. He not only offered Himself up to be sacrificed, but He was also the first

The world doesn't mind a Christian going to church on Sunday as long as that same Christian doesn't stand for righteousness in the marketplace, as long as he or she doesn't make waves during the week. . . . The world will go along with partial sacrifices, but God only accepts complete ones.

"living" sacrifice. He was placed on the altar of Calvary alive. And when He died, His was the last death that would ever be made for sin, because the death of this "living" sacrifice paid for sin once for all.

Since that day it is a live offering that God is waiting on, that God accepts. But even in presenting our bodies as living sacrifices, we are dying to ourselves because in the very presenting of the sacrifice is the act of surrender. And the more we die to self, the more alive we become to God. Dying to self and living to God take place as we keep ourselves on the altar. That is why we must be ever vigilant to do so. Presenting ourselves as living sacrifices is not a one-time event, nor is being "filled with the Spirit" (Eph. 5:18) a one-time happening. It is a continuous process. Keep on being filled. Keep on presenting ourselves.

3. ***The sacrifice we make will be a holy one.*** The offering, Paul says, is to be "holy and pleasing to God" (Rom. 12:1). Under the Old Covenant the sacrifices were to be without blemish. Let's read again what the psalmist said in Psalm 24:3-4, "Who may ascend the hill of the Lord? Who may stand in his holy place? He who has clean hands and a pure heart, who does not lift up his soul to an idol or swear by what is false."

The living sacrifice that is acceptable to God is one that has, first of all, been cleansed by the blood of the Savior at salvation and is continually being cleansed through confession and repentance on the part of the worshiper. "If we [continually] confess our sins, he is faithful and just and will [continually] forgive us our sins and [continually] purify us from all unrighteousness" (1 John 1:9). Forgiveness and cleansing are the preparations for a holy sacrifice.

4. ***The sacrifice we make will be an acceptable one.*** Here we find it again, just as we did on day 2 in 1 Peter 2:5, where the apostle spoke of offering spiritual sacrifices in accordance with, or what was acceptable to, God through Jesus Christ. This last point leads into what we will be discussing in more detail on day 5 of this week, but we need to point out here that we don't offer this living sacrifice in a haphazard way. Just as thought and preparation went into the sacrifices in the Old Testament, so today we must give thought to meeting God's conditions for this offering. All of this adds up to our presenting to God that which He desires from us, a living offering that pleases Him.

5. ***The sacrifice will be a transforming one.*** The ultimate purpose for this living sacrifice, other than giving to God that which He is due, is what it will do to us and for us. The result of this act of worship will be the transforming of the character of the worshiper, the one who is making the offering. No one who truly worships will ever be the same again.

The ultimate purpose for this living sacrifice, other than giving to God that which He is due, is what it will do to us and for us. The result of this act of worship will be the transforming of the character of the worshiper, the one who is making the offering.

There are no shortcuts with God. But, oh, the joy when we prepare and present the worship offering that is pleasing to God—when, holding nothing back, we place our all on the altar.

It is interesting how Paul ties the living sacrifice itself to the effect it will have upon the maker of the sacrifice. It will have an effect on:

Our minds—You recall what the apostle Paul said in his letter to the church at Philippi: "Let this mind be in you, which was also in Christ Jesus" (Phil. 2:5, KJV). Our minds will be renewed as we daily present our bodies as living sacrifices to God. Little by little we will be transforming into the likeness of our Lord. We will become less and less like the world, not be conformed to this world (Rom. 12:2) and more and more like Jesus.

> His love in me loving, His mind in me thinking,
>   His life in me living through the Spirit's power.
> His eyes in me seeing, His heart in me beating,
>   His voice through me speaking every waking hour.
>
> —Ron & Patricia Owens © 1986

The offering of our bodies as living sacrifices results in the mind and life of our Lord being more and more operative in us.

Knowing and understanding of God's will for our lives—How many of God's children are struggling to know what God's will is, not realizing that until they place themselves on the altar, they will not know His good and acceptable and perfect will for them (Rom. 12:1-2). The more consistent we are in keeping our "bodies" on the altar, the more conformed we will be to Christ and the more we will be able to discern what it is that God intends for us.

> This place O Lord, the altar; the offering, my life—
>   My body, Lord, I give to you, a living sacrifice.
> Lord I surrender all my rights, my will, my talents too—
>   Lord, not a thing would I hold back, I yield my all to you.
>
> —Ron & Patricia Owens © 1986

There are no shortcuts with God. But, oh, the joy when we prepare and present the worship offering that is pleasing to God—when, holding nothing back, we place our all on the altar. It is then that we will experience God's transforming and renewing work in our minds and hearts. It is then that we will know, and joyfully do, His will.

Read Romans 12:1-2 once more. List the five things found there that describe the worshiper's becoming the worship offering.

1. _____

2. _____

3. _____

4. _____

5. _____

Therefore, I urge you, brothers, in view of God's mercy, to offer your bodies as living sacrifices, holy and pleasing to God—this is your spiritual act of worship. Do not conform any longer to the pattern of this world, but be transformed by the renewing of your mind. Then you will be able to test and approve what God's will is—his good, pleasing and perfect will.

— Romans 12:1-2

"Give, and it will be given to you. A good measure, pressed down, shaken together and running over, will be poured into your lap. For with the measure you use, it will be measured to you."

— Luke 6:38

Day 4: Are You a Getter or a Giver?

As we have seen many times already in this study, worship is an offering; it is an act of giving. It will mean the gift of time. The person who worships sports will give both time and money to fulfill his desire to worship. A person who worships a boat or a car will give all the time and money needed to fulfill that need to worship. A person who worships a career and money will give all the time and effort needed to get what he or she wants. Giving is at the heart of worship.

When it comes to worshiping God, is that how you feel? Do you go to church looking forward to joining other worshipers in the offering of yourself to God in worship, or do you go, as many do today, thinking only of what you will get, how much you will enjoy yourself? Explain.

_____

_____

_____

_____

_____

In the western world we live in a society that is dominated by commercialism and consumerism. Shopping has become a game of multiple choice. The advertising media greatly influences us to buy certain products. But this is no longer just confined to the things of the world; it has entered the life of the church. The same spirit of competition that drives our Western economy now drives a large portion of today's church. From billboards to newspapers, churches are advertising and offering people what they hope will be unique, something that will appeal to consumer tastes, something they may not find in another "competing" church. And so, some Christians, moving into a community or having become dissatisfied with the church they presently attend, begin to "shop" for a church, looking for one that will give them what they want.

Many see the church primarily as being there for them, rather than a body to which God desires to add them, so they can worship and serve Him with, and through, that congregation of believers.

What did you see in the church you attend when you first began attending it? Why did you join the church you are now in?

_____

_____

_____

But isn't the Christian life one of receiving as well? Of course it is. Our life with God began with our receiving from Him the gift of eternal life. "God so loved the world that he gave" (John 3:16). And God's giving to His children does not end there. In fact, God delights in blessing His people. He delights in pouring out the blessings He has promised us "in the heavenly realms with every spiritual blessing in Christ" (Eph. 1:3). Just as the transforming of our thinking and living is a result of the offering of our bodies, so does God's goodness and mercy follow us all the days of our lives when we are walking in His will. A major part of our lives is enjoying God and the blessings He gives.

However, God does not bless or give indiscriminately. Why? Because God never violates His character. Therefore the blessings we receive from Him are contingent on our meeting His conditions for blessing. Let's read Luke 6:38 again. "Give, and it will be given to you. A good measure, pressed down, shaken together and running over, will be poured into your lap. For with the measure you use, it will be measured to you." What a promise! But notice the condition. Giving precedes receiving.

With this in mind, in light of what worship is—an offering, an act of giving—suppose God were to lead you to a church that humanly speaking would not be your first choice, a place where you would not be getting all that you would like to get, but a place, nevertheless, where God had chosen to put you for His purposes? What if the music of this church was not "your kind?" What if _____ ? You fill in the blank.

What would you do if this were the case?

_____

_____

Just as the transforming of our thinking and living is a result of the offering of our bodies, so does God's goodness and mercy follow us all the days of our lives when we are walking in His will.

I wonder how often we miss what God wants to do in our lives because we are primarily thinking about receiving rather than giving?

When my wife and I (Ron) first moved to Atlanta, God led us to join a dying, inner-city church that was 45 miles from where we lived. If it were not for the definite prompting of the Holy Spirit, we would not have gone there. But He had a purpose in this, one of which was that He wanted to teach us some things that we could not have otherwise learned if we had only looked for what we could get from a church. I wonder how often we miss what God wants to do in our lives because we are primarily thinking about receiving rather than giving?

Remember the story of King David and Araunah? David wanted to purchase his threshing floor from him to build an altar on, and when Araunah offered to give it to the king at no charge, David replied: "I insist on paying you for it. I will not sacrifice to the Lord my God burnt offerings that cost me nothing" (2 Sam. 24:24).

Isaac Watts expressed this attitude of heart so beautifully in his hymn "When I Survey the Wondrous Cross." The last stanza says:

Were the whole realm of nature mine,
That were an offering far too small;
Love so amazing, so divine,
Demands my soul, my life, my all.

His original word was *offering*, not *present*, as it may be found in your hymnal. He understood what Paul was talking about in Romans 12:1. He understood that worship is the offering of all we are to the One we worship. God is waiting for those whom He has redeemed to offer Him a "living sacrifice." Acceptable worship requires this kind of sacrifice. "Abraham built an altar there and arranged the wood on it. He bound his son Isaac and laid him on the altar" (Gen. 22:9). Identity with Christ and His death is key, so that we can give Him the living sacrifice of our lives.

Day 5: Are You Accepted or Rejected?

Though our personal acceptance by God is based on what Christ has done for us, not on our performance, He does evaluate and judge our offerings, either accepting or rejecting them. This is most important because it not only affects our future in our earthly life, but it will also affect our future in eternity.

Having looked at God's standard for worship and the kind of offering He seeks, let us ask God to help us personally allow the light of His truth to shine into our souls. This is important because making the adjustments we need to make will determine whether our worship will be acceptable to Him. There is worship that is acceptable to God, and there is worship that is unacceptable.

One of the dominating themes of Scripture is the worship of God, and since man was made for worship, he reaches his greatest potential when he himself becomes the kind of worshiper God wants, the kind of worshiper who can offer God worship that is acceptable. Failure to understand what God is looking for leads to the attempt to substitute counterfeits for the real thing and ultimately having the worship offering we present rejected.

The psalmist David lived with the sensitivity that what he offered might well be unacceptable to God. He realized that the attitude of his heart would determine whether God would look with favor on what he brought to the altar. There were soul-searching moments in David's life as he asked God to search his heart. "Search me, O God, and know my heart; test me and know my anxious thoughts. See if there is any offensive way in me, and lead me in the way everlasting" (Ps. 139:23-24).

In Psalm 27:9, he prayed, "Do not hide your face from me, do not turn your servant away in anger; you have been my helper. Do not reject me or forsake me, O God my Savior."

Reflect on the message of Psalm 139:23-24 and Psalm 27:9. What do these verses say about what God requires the attitude of our hearts to be?

_____

_____

_____

> The Lord looked with favor on Abel and his offering, but on Cain and his offering he did not look with favor.
>
> — Genesis 4:4-5

> Search me, O God, and know my heart; test me and know my anxious thoughts. See if there is any offensive way in me, and lead me in the way everlasting.
>
> — Psalm 139:23-24

> Do not hide your face from me, do not turn your servant away in anger; you have been my helper. Do not reject me or forsake me, O God my Savior.
>
> — Psalm 27:9

In the first chapter of Isaiah, we find God's people going through all the prescribed forms of worship, offering the sacrifices in the way God had instructed them to do, careful to observe the law outwardly, yet what they were doing was rejected by God. "Stop bringing meaningless offerings!" He said. "Your incense is detestable to me. New Moons, Sabbaths and convocations—I cannot bear your evil assemblies. Your New Moon festivals and your appointed feasts my soul hates. They have become a burden to me; I am weary of bearing them. When you spread out your hands in prayer, I will hide my eyes from you; even if you offer many prayers, I will not listen" (Isa. 1:13-15).

Why did God reject what they were offering Him? In a nutshell it was because it was not coming from the heart, and it was totally contrary to everything God stood for. They would worship the gods of the nations around them, then they would come into God's house and worship Him. They thought that as long as they took the time to worship God He would not mind their worshiping a few other gods as well. After all, they were fulfilling their duty. The offering that God looks on with favor, however, is the offering that springs from a heart that loves Him supremely and worships Him exclusively!

As we bring this week to a close, look back over the preceding four lessons and make two lists, a list of those things that will cause your worship to be accepted by God and a list of those things that would cause God to reject what you offer Him. After making these lists, prayerfully place them against your own life and worship. If you find yourself in the second list, take time to present what you find to God and ask Him to help you repent and make the necessary adjustments so that your worship offering will be acceptable to Him.

Worship God Accepts   Worship God Rejects

_____ _____

_____ _____

_____ _____

_____ _____

_____ _____

_____ _____

_____ _____

The Lifestyle of a Transformed Worshiper

Brother Lawrence lived over three hundred years ago. His life still touches ours today through the little book *Practicing the Presence of God.* As he was lying on his deathbed, those who were attending him were surprised to hear him say, "I am not dying." One of them asked, "Then, Brother Lawrence, what are you doing?" His reply was, "I am doing what I have been doing all my life; I am worshiping the God I love." He knew why God had created him, and it was not long before he entered into the presence of the One he loved to worship Him throughout eternity.

Worship is a lifestyle. It is in fact, "practicing the presence of God all day long." You are a worshiper, not just when you go to church, but every moment you live. It was for this reason God made you in the first place. He desires your love and worship. This week we are going to be looking at the lives of people who understood this.

Key Verse
And we, who with unveiled faces all reflect the Lord's glory, are being transformed into his likeness with ever-increasing glory, which comes from the Lord, who is the Spirit.
— 2 Corinthians 3:18

This Week's Lessons

1. Worship and the Common Person
2. Worship in the Home
3. Worship in the Workplace
4. Worship in National Life
5. Worship in Spiritual Leadership

Day 1: Worship and the Common Person

John 4:22-24 says, "You Samaritans worship what you do not know; we worship what we do know, for salvation is from the Jews. Yet a time is coming and has now come when the true worshipers will worship the Father in spirit and truth, for they are the kind of worshipers the Father seeks. God is spirit, and his worshipers must worship in spirit and in truth."

Once again we find our Lord touching the "common" person. He especially wanted this ordinary sinner, the woman at the well, who lived in Sychar, to know how life-changing worship, true worship, could be for her.

Speaking truthfully, Jesus told her that she had never known or experienced true worship (John 4:22). He was saying, "You worship, but you do not experience God transforming your Life!"

Jesus answered her that "a time is coming and has now come when the true worshipers will worship the Father in spirit and truth" (v. 23). He, who was God in the flesh, was now inviting her to experience right then, face-to-face with God, true life-transforming worship. In Jesus' presence she pursued the right questions and was given a life-changing answer. This is always what happens when true worship is taking place. The heart is pursuing God for life-changing truth.

There came to this common woman worship's transformational moment: "When he [the Messiah] comes, he will explain everything to us" (v. 25). Then she heard personally from God, in Christ, a truth that set her free: "I who speak to you am he" (v. 26). In an instant her whole life was transformed by an encounter with God in Christ, and she left everything to run back to the city to tell her friends. This is true worship in the life of a common person. Worship at its finest!

The woman at the well was looking for the Messiah to come. Her lifestyle, however, hardened her heart in her search. Jesus renewed her desire for a Savior. List four people who need you to kindle their desire for a Savior.

1. _____

2. _____

3. _____

4. _____

Describe how open you are to Christ's speaking through you and a lifestyle of worship to reach these people you have listed.

_____

_____

_____

_____

God takes ordinary, common people—where they are—and brings them into a life-changing encounter with Himself, enabling them to worship "in spirit and in truth."

Worship is when one comes face-to-face with God. That place immediately becomes holy ground for God is present, as happened with Moses in Exodus 3:4-6. Throughout the Bible the place of personal worship could be anywhere:

- Abraham when God called him to leave home and relatives (Gen. 12:1-8)
- Joshua on a hill overlooking Jericho (Josh. 5:13-15)
- Isaiah in the temple (Isa. 6:1-9)
- Amos while he was herding sheep and tending sycamore trees (Amos 7:14-16)
- Joseph and Mary, very common peasant people, probably in their homes—Joseph while he was sleeping (Matt. 1:18-25) and Mary (Luke 1:26-38)
- Peter, James, and John while they were cleaning their fishing nets (Luke 5:1-11)
- John exiled on the Isle of Patmos, on the Lord's Day while he meditated (Rev. 1:9-11)

God takes ordinary, common people—where they are—and brings them into a life-changing encounter with Himself, enabling them to worship "in spirit and in truth." This was especially true with another "common" person whose story we find in Matthew 26:6-13. It takes place in the home of a common person in Bethan, where Jesus and His disciples had been invited to eat. Lazarus, whom Jesus had raised from the dead was there, as were his sisters, Mary and Martha.

After the meal, Mary, who had been listening to Jesus talk, went and got a bottle of perfume that she had been saving, no doubt as a part of her dowry. It was very expensive perfume. She then did a shocking thing. She knelt at the feet of Jesus, broke the bottle, and began pouring it over His feet. Her next move was perhaps even more astounding, and it caused everyone watching to gasp. She committed a serious breach

Worship is an attitude

before it becomes an act,

and an act of worship

without an accompanying

heart attitude of devotion

to our Lord is unacceptable

to Him.

of public etiquette by undoing her hair and wiping Jesus' feet with it. Judas became incensed over what he called a terrible waste of money that could have been used for the poor, though he was thinking only of padding his own pockets. But Jesus knew exactly what was taking place and He said: "Leave her alone, . . . [It was intended] that she should save this perfume for the day of my burial. You will always have the poor among you, but you will not always have me" (John 12:7-8).

We can learn several lessons from this beautiful act of worship on the part of one of God's common people. Let's look at them.

What Mary did revealed what was in her heart. Worship is the expression of our heart's devotion, and Mary loved her Lord more than anything or anyone else. Worship is an attitude before it becomes an act, and an act of worship without an accompanying heart attitude of devotion to our Lord is unacceptable to Him.

A true "heart attitude" of worship will always find a way of expressing itself outwardly. As Mary watched her Lord and listened to what he was saying during that meal, she was so overwhelmed with love for her Master that she began wondering what she could do to express this love for Him. In all likelihood He had been preparing them for what was going to happen to Him in a little more than a week, because He alluded to His burial in response to her sacrifice.

While the others sat there, Mary slipped away. She had suddenly thought of what would be the most profound expression of her love, what would be the ultimate act of worship, what would be the greatest sacrifice in light of what He was going to do for her, and she poured it over the feet of her Lord. Her heart would let her do nothing less. She had to act on what was inside.

Someone has pointed out that worship is a verb and that whenever it is mentioned in Scripture it is found in the context of action. True worship in the heart will always find a corresponding outward expression. Love that is not expressed is not love. Love must be given away. Mary's action was one of unrestrained love. She could not hold it in.

What is your "rare bottle of perfume," and how could you offer it in love to the Master?

_____

_____

_____

Mary's act was one of deep and honest humility. She was unashamed to let everyone know how much she loved her Master. She bowed before Him. She knelt at His feet and wiped them with her hair.

It is interesting to note that whenever we find this Mary mentioned in the Bible she is always at the feet of Jesus. She was not embarrassed. She risked ridicule and criticism which she had on another occasion received from her sister, Martha, and now from one of Jesus' disciples. But that didn't matter to Mary. Her favorite place was at the feet of her Lord.

What a testimony and example for us all! Is that where we would prefer to be? Are we ready to humble ourselves? Are we willing to bear the criticism of acquaintances and relatives? Reflect on these questions and note your thoughts here.

_____

_____

_____

Mary's act was the expression of great sacrifice. She gave "lavishly." She gave, in all probability, what she was saving as a treasure for here marriage dowry, the most precious thing she possessed, worth the wages for an entire year's labor. (Today that would translate to at least $25,000).

She did not hesitate to give that which would cost her the most. She did not pour just a small amount on His feet. She held nothing back. She used the whole bottle in her worship. Is that how we feel when we worship? Or are we guilty of holding back, of going to church and pouring only a few drops of sacrifice out before the Lord while reserving the remainder of the bottle for ourselves?

Mary's worship had an affect on her and on others. Though our motive in worshiping is not to get for ourselves but to give to God, we, the worshipers, are always the recipients of His blessing beyond anything we could imagine. Mary carried the fragrance of her worship with her for days to come. It was on her hands, it was in her hair, it was everywhere she went—the aroma of a worshiper! She had made the sacrifice of worship, and she carried the result of that sacrifice with her. But she was not the only one affected by what she had done. Everyone in the house that day was touched by the aroma of Mary's worship. The fragrance of her offering was an unmistakable testimony to her love for

Though our motive in worshiping is not to get for ourselves but to give to God, we, the worshipers, are always the recipients of His blessing beyond anything we could imagine.

Jesus. Not everyone is going to respond positively, as was the case with Judas, but those around us will be affected one way or another by the life and witness of a true worshiper.

In Ephesians 5:1-2, Paul admonishes the church at Ephesus to "be imitators of God, therefore, as dearly loved children and live a life of love, just as Christ loved us and gave himself up for us as a fragrant offering and sacrifice to God." Every true sacrifice, every true act of worship not only rises to God as a sweet smelling aroma, but the aroma of our worship affects others. Jesus preserved the worship of Mary. He honored the worship of this common woman when He said: "I tell you the truth, wherever this gospel is preached throughout the world, what she has done will also be told, in memory of her" (Matt. 26:13). The aroma of Mary's worship is still affecting us today.

Mary's worship pleased God. This is the ultimate test. We may please ourselves, and we may please others with how we worship, but the question we must always be asking ourselves is, "Is what I am doing, pleasing to God?" This is the most important thing.

Mary seemed to understand Jesus better than all the others there that day. She had heard Him speak of His death, and she was immediately ready to anoint His body. What were the others doing? They were sitting there listening and watching but doing nothing. Did they love Jesus? To a degree they did. Other than Judas, most of the other disciples would ultimately lay down their lives for their Lord, but that day, recorded for us in history, Mary was the only one who put her worship into action. The worship of a common person in the middle of life's routine.

Day 2: Worship in the Home

Some of us use the term *family worship* to describe significant moments when the family, together or separately, have a life-transforming encounter with God. It can be in a regular devotional time, in a specially planned seasonal time such as Thanksgiving or Christmas. It can be while praying before going to sleep, alone or with a parent.

When the heart turns to meet God and all the senses are focused on Him, worship is real and transforming. Many children have placed saving faith in Jesus Christ in the home. Many have secured their call to missions in the home. Many, together in the home, have encountered God in deep repentance and returned to God having heard a parent or a grandparent in prayer or having watched them pour over the Scripture with tears. The home is a God-appointed place for worship. Not only that, but true worship at home creates great readiness to worship at church or with any other corporate gathering of believers.

It is obvious that young Timothy developed a life of faith from his home. So real was Timothy's faith that Paul chose him to be his companion on his missionary journeys. Paul knew of his home when he reminded Timothy: "I have been reminded of your sincere faith, which first lived in your grandmother Lois and in your mother Eunice and, I am persuaded, now lives in you also" (2 Tim. 1:5). God was regularly encountered in Timothy's home, and this left a legacy of faith in God in his life.

Both of us (Ron and Henry) can bear true witness to godly worship in our homes. Many moments changed our lives forever, encountering God and His will while in worship in our homes. This legacy drove both of us to make formal and informal times of worship a vital part of our homes, greatly influencing all of our children. We now see worship in our children's homes and rejoice!

It must be noted that Abram "built an altar" almost everywhere he lived, and I believe we can safely say it was not only for himself but for his family as well. This pattern of building an altar in the home was repeated in Isaac's life, especially when God spoke to Him and made a covenant with him (Gen. 26:24-25). This pattern of family worship was important in Isaac's son Jacob (Gen. 33:20). Worship in home life was important to God, as he later instructed Jacob, "Go up to Bethel and settle there, and build an altar there to God, who appeared to you" (Gen. 35:1; read also Gen. 28:10-22).

When the heart turns to meet God and all the senses are focused on Him, worship is real and transforming.

About midnight Paul and Silas were praying and singing hymns to God, and the other prisoners were listening to them. Suddenly there was such a violent earthquake that the foundations of the prison were shaken. At once all the prison doors flew open, and everybody's chains came loose. The jailer woke up, and when he saw the prison doors open, he drew his sword and was about to kill himself because he thought the prisoners had escaped. But Paul shouted, "Don't harm yourself! We are all here!" The jailer called for lights, rushed in and fell trembling before Paul and Silas. He then brought them out and asked, "Sirs, what must I do to be saved?" They replied, "Believe in the Lord Jesus, and you will be saved—you and your household." Then they spoke the word of the Lord to him and to all the others in his house.

— Acts 16:25-33

Answer the following and prayerfully consider your responses:

___ Have you made worship a vital part of your home?

___ Do you expect life-changing encounters with God in your home?

___ Do your children notice your worship in the home, and are you sharing what God is saying together? Why or why not?

_____

___ Does God meet you regularly, in the formal and informal moments of worship in your home?

Now, as we conclude today's study, read the following Scriptures, and as you do, look for the role the home had as a training ground for worship.

- Cornelius' home (Acts 10:1-48)
- The Philippian jailer's home (Acts 16:24-36)
- Dorcas' home (Acts 9:36-42)
- Lydia's home (Acts 16:11-15)
- The home of Aquilla and Priscilla (Rom. 16:3; 1 Cor. 16:19; 2 Tim. 4:19)

Day 3: Worship in the Workplace

Most of the encounters with God throughout Scripture took place in the workplace, or marketplace. This is obviously a choice God makes. The process, or way of God, for such a worship encounter with God has the following elements:

1. God takes the initiative to come to His people in their workplace and invites them to respond to His presence.
2. There is then a clear face-to-face encounter with God, where God makes known His activity or purpose in their lives.
3. God communicates truth, usually accompanied by a clear command or direction.
4. The person in His presence makes a choice to obey God's command.
5. God does a work that reveals Himself to the person, that he or she is never the same again.
6. The worshiper continues in this personal relationship with God and God's invitation, so that he or she is now involved with God as He completes His purposes (transformation) in and through the individual (usually some aspect of redemption).

One of the clearest New Testament witnesses to this process in worship in the workplace is Peter (and with him, James and John), in Luke 5:1-11.

In Luke 5:1-3, Jesus came to where Peter and his friends were fishing, and now cleaning their nets. He had "stood" and "seen" Peter's boat and deliberately chose to get into his boat, put out a little from the land (with Peter), and began to teach truth from the Father to the multitudes—and to Peter.

Having finished teaching, Jesus deliberately turned to Peter and began to get Peter involved with Him and who His is and what He had in mind for Peter. Worship always involves this aspect—inviting people to respond to Him.

Jesus had taught truth and now wanted Peter to apply it to his own life. Little did Peter know what God had in mind for his life. Worship is always like this. Jesus taught truth about the Father and His kingdom, and how near it all was now for Peter. The truth of God (gospel, or good news of God) would require a personal response of faith. Worship always creates such a moment. Then truth was accompanied by a command from Jesus: "Put out into deep water, and let down the nets for a catch" (v. 4). Worship in the workplace requires faith—in the workplace, with your colleagues watching.

When he had finished speaking, he said to Simon, "Put out into deep water, and let down the nets for a catch." Simon answered, "Master, we've worked hard all night and haven't caught anything. But because you say so, I will let down the nets." When they had done so, they caught such a large number of fish that their nets began to break. So they signaled their partners in the other boat to come and help them, and they came and filled both boats so full that they began to sink. When Simon Peter saw this, he fell at Jesus' knees and said, "Go away from me, Lord; I am a sinful man!" For he and all his companions were astonished at the catch of fish they had taken, and so were James and John the sons of Zebedee, Simon's partners. Then Jesus said to Simon, "Don't be afraid; from now on you will catch men."

— Luke 5:4-10

Peter obeyed, though he had only the word he had heard from Jesus. It was a choice he had to make. It would be based on what he now knew while in Jesus' presence.

Suddenly, a catch of fish! No, much more! Suddenly God revealed Himself uniquely to Peter, in the workplace, and in a way he could understand.

Peter was forever changed while face-to-face with God in his workplace. "Go away from me, Lord; I am a sinful man!" (v. 8). The change had taken place. The sinner was in the presence of the Lord.

Jesus now invites Peter to release *all* of his life to Him, as a worthy offering to his Lord, and assures Peter of a new "career," catching men.

Read Luke 5:4-10. God revealed Himself and His activity to Simon Peter. In what ways has God shown Himself to you and invited you to join Him in His work where you work?

_____

_____

_____

The rest of Peter's life is recorded in the Gospels, the Book of Acts, and 1 and 2 Peter. Worship in the workplace is totally life transforming. Do you expect to worship, at God's invitation, in your workplace?

_____

Would you:
___ Hear Him as He teaches you there?
___ Obey when He commands?
___ And obey your Lord before your colleagues?

Why or why not?

_____

_____

_____

Day 4: Worship in National Life

Some of the deepest moments of worship for God's people came in their national life. There is a dimension of worship that can only be experienced "nationally"—that is, the whole people of God, in their national setting, standing in the presence of Holy God. There, before Him, God reveals Himself, and His people respond in brokenness, repentance, trembling, and obedience. When God calls for, or initiates a solemn assembly for His people, the potential is for great revival among His people and spiritual awakening in the lost (including surrounding nations—even globally).

The first, and most dramatic worship experience nationally, was when God revealed Himself to His people at Mt. Sinai in Exodus 19–20. Let's look at several special features in national worship that are revealed in God's Word!

1. Such a gathering is by God's invitation, and often, by His command.
2. God gives guidance to His leaders for how the people should come before Him.
3. Cleansing is a necessary preparation by all the people.
4. All, including the children, are to come to worship, with no exceptions.
5. The encounter with God is real, personal, and corporate,
6. The fear of God usually accompanies national worship.
7. Scripture (Word from God) and prayer are prominent.
8. God always has a specific objective in mind for his people.
9. God's people repent corporately, and great forgiveness is followed by great blessing.
10. God is greatly glorified in His people, not only before His own people but also before a watching world.

Consider the list of 10 special features of national worship. Note any indication of these activities of God you may see or wish to pray for in your country.

_____

_____

_____

_____

When God calls for, or initiates a solemn assembly for His people, the potential is for great revival among His people and spiritual awakening in the lost (including surrounding nations—even globally).

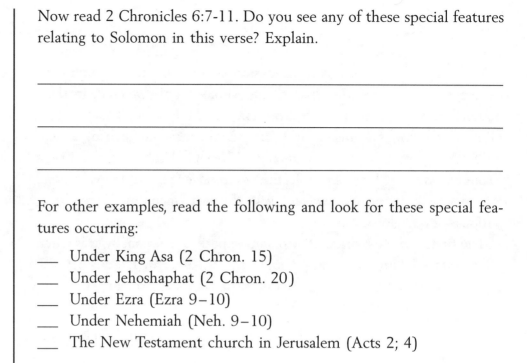

> "My father David had it in his heart to build a temple for the Name of the Lord, the God of Israel. But the Lord said to my father David, 'Because it was in your heart to build a temple for my Name, you did well to have this in your heart. Nevertheless, you are not the one to build the temple, but your son, who is your own flesh and blood—he is the one who will build the temple for my Name.' The Lord has kept the promise he made. I have succeeded David my father and now I sit on the throne of Israel, just as the Lord promised, and I have built the temple for the Name of the Lord, the God of Israel. There I have placed the ark, in which is the covenant of the Lord that he made with the people of Israel."
>
> 2 Chronicles 6:7-11

Now read 2 Chronicles 6:7-11. Do you see any of these special features relating to Solomon in this verse? Explain.

_____

_____

_____

For other examples, read the following and look for these special features occurring:

___ Under King Asa (2 Chron. 15)
___ Under Jehoshaphat (2 Chron. 20)
___ Under Ezra (Ezra 9–10)
___ Under Nehemiah (Neh. 9–10)
___ The New Testament church in Jerusalem (Acts 2; 4)

In every case the lifestyle of the worshipers was radically changed! God's people dramatically changed how they were living. True worship always transforms individuals, families, workplaces, and nations!

In Exodus 19–20, we find God revealing a pattern for national worship in His people.

First, He suddenly commanded Moses to stand before Him on Mt. Sinai and commanded Moses to gather His people on a certain day, in a certain way, for a certain purpose. God would make a solemn covenant with His people, to establish them as "His people" and He would be "their God."

Second, God gave the instructions to the leader He had chosen. He told Moses exactly what to say to the people when they gathered (the Word of God), and how to prepare them.

Third, in Exodus 19:10-11, God told them to cleanse themselves for three days in preparation for meeting their Holy God. It was very specific. Cleansing always precedes national worship.

Fourth, God commands all His people to come; no one is to be free not to come. So serious and important is this to God that King Asa declared, "Whosoever would not seek the Lord God of Israel should be put to death" (2 Chron. 15:13, KJV). Whenever God summons for national worship, it is a serious moment.

Fifth and sixth, in the encounter with God on Sinai, all the people witnessed God's awful presence and "they trembled and stood at a distance" (Ex. 20:18-21, NASB). It records that God's presence nationally is of such a nature, "for God has come in order to test you, and in order that the fear of Him may remain with you, so that you may not sin" (Ex 20:20, NASB). In Solomon's day, when God's presence "filled the temple," 2 Chronicles records the people's response: "When all the children of Israel saw how the fire came down, and the glory of the Lord upon the house, they bowed themselves with their faces to the ground upon the pavement, and worshipped, and praised the Lord" (2 Chron. 7:3, KJV).

In times of great revival, the presence of God brings awesome and profound responses from those present (see Brian Edwards' book, *Revival! A People Saturated with God*, Evangelical Press).

Seventh, they had given to them a specific word from God (Ex 19:3-8). In Nehemiah's day, "they stood . . . and read from the Book of the Law of the Lord their God for a quarter of the day" (Neh. 9:3).

Eighth, God had in mind a solemn covenant be made with His people under Moses. Global redemption was underway. This is always God's purpose in national worship. In times of great revival, God always purposes to turn an entire nation back to Himself, and through them to touch the world. This was true of the great revival in America in 1857–59 and of nation-shaking revivals in Ireland, Scotland, and many other nations of the world.

Ninth, God's people, nationally repented, were cleansed and entered fully into a covenant with God, and God heard them and blessed them.

Tenth, in completed national worship, God is always exalted and glorified in the eyes of this people, and a watching world.

Process and record your thoughts as statements of more than one word:

Are you ready for God to command you, and your church, to meet with great numbers of His people to worship, seek His face, and trust Him for His blessing?

_____

Are you and your people walking in the fear of God sufficiently that you would insist every member of your family and church be present?

_____

Do you want God once again to be exalted and glorified in your nation?

_____

In times of great revival, God always purposes to turn an entire nation back to Himself, and through them to touch a world.

Righteousness exalts a
nation, but sin is a
disgrace to any people.
— Proverbs 14:34

There were several times in the history of the United States when, seeing what was happening in the land, the president and congress called the entire nation to humble themselves before the mighty hand of God, to confess national sins, and plead the mercy of God. Though not every citizen would have cooperated, unlike what was "required" by God of His chosen people, nevertheless much of the land went to their knees.

Read the following declaration of President Lincoln who so strongly believed that "righteousness exalts a nation, but sin is a disgrace to any people" (Prov. 14:34). As you read, those of you who are from the United States of America, do you gain a sense of how far Americans have turned away from being a nation that once acknowledged the supremacy of God, that bowed before Him, and might we even say, that "worshiped" Him?

It is fit and becoming in all people, at all times, to acknowledge and revere the Supreme Government of God; to bow in humble submission to His chastisement; to confess and deplore their sins and transgressions in the full conviction that the fear of the Lord is the beginning of wisdom; and to pray, with all fervency and contrition, for the pardon of their past offenses, and for a blessing upon their present and prospective action.

We have been the recipients of the choicest bounties of heaven. We have been preserved these many years in peace and prosperity. We have grown in numbers, wealth and power as no nation has ever grown. But, we have forgotten God. We have forgotten the gracious hand that has preserved us in peace, and multiplied and enriched and strengthened us; and we have vainly imagined, in the deceitfulness of our hearts, that all these blessings were produced by some superior wisdom and virtue of own.

Intoxicated with unbroken success, we have become too self-sufficient to feel the necessity of redeeming and preserving grace, too proud to pray to the God who made us.

It behooves us then to humble ourselves before the offended Power, to confess our national sins and to pray for clemency and forgiveness.

Now, therefore, in compliance with the request and fully concurring in the view of the Senate, I do, by this proclamation designate and set apart Thursday the 30th of April 1863, as a day of national humiliation, fasting and prayer.

Day 5: Worship in Spiritual Leadership

The apostle Paul was a worshiper. His epistles are saturated with expressions of his own worship as well as teaching and admonition to the churches and to his son in the ministry, Timothy, on worship. Every letter he wrote, every prayer he prayed, every sermon he preached, issued from the heart of a worshiper. He had encountered God in such a dramatic way on the road to Damascus that he, like Isaiah, never wavered in his commitment to serve and worship his Lord.

As goes the worship of spiritual leaders, so goes the worship of God's people. A most astounding passage of Scripture awaits us today. It reveals and deals with the effect of the worship of spiritual leaders on God's people. The spiritual leader's personal relationship with God, for good or for bad, dramatically affects not only the worship of God's people but also their way of life.

Moses was called and assigned by God to be a spiritual leader for His people. This required that Moses know God intimately, and he did. So we read: "The Lord would speak to Moses face to face, as a man speaks with his friend" (Ex. 33:11). So when God's people grievously sinned against God by making a golden calf to worship, Moses made a pleading intercession for them. God heard his cry and spared the people. But the description of Moses' worship and its affect on the people is dramatic: "Now Moses used to take a tent and pitch it outside the camp some distance away, calling it the 'tent of meeting.' Anyone inquiring of the Lord would go to the tent of meeting outside the camp. And whenever Moses went out to the tent, all the people rose and stood at the entrances to their tents, watching Moses until he entered the tent. As Moses went into the tent, the pillar of cloud would come down and stay at the entrance, while the Lord spoke with Moses. Whenever the people saw the pillar of cloud standing at the entrance to the tent, they all stood and worshiped, each at the entrance to his tent." (Ex. 33:7-10).

When Moses worshiped, the people worshiped. They realized that as went Moses' time before God so went their own life. This was true. Listen to part of the worship experience of Moses as he pleads with God. Then hear God's reply:

"Moses bowed to the ground at once and worshiped. 'O Lord, if I have found favor in your eyes,' he said, 'then let the Lord go with us. Although this is a stiff-necked people, forgive our wickedness and our sin, and take us as your inheritance.'

"Then the Lord said: 'I am making a covenant with you. Before all your people I will do wonders never before done in any nation in all

The spiritual leader's personal relationship with God, for good or for bad, dramatically affects not only the worship of God's people but also their way of life.

the world. The people you live among will see how awesome is the work that I, the Lord, will do for you'" (Ex. 34:8-10).

As Moses walked with the Lord in worship, so went the worship of the people of God—and so went the activity of God toward His people. This same truth is seen in Malachi 3:2-4: "But who can endure the day of His coming? Who can stand when He appears? For He will be like a refiner's fire or a launderer's soap. He will sit as a refiner and a purifier of silver; he will purify the Levites and refine them like gold and silver. Then the Lord will have men who will bring offerings in righteousness, and the offerings of Judah and Jerusalem will be acceptable to the Lord, as in days gone by, as in former years."

Read Malachi 3:2-4. Verse 2 describes God's refining power with common examples for those times. Rephrase this passage with an example of purifying substances today.

_____

_____

_____

When God comes in revival presence, He will first deal strongly with the "Levites" (the spiritual leaders). When they, as refined spiritual leaders, "bring offerings in righteousness, and the offerings of Judah and Jerusalem [the people of God] will be acceptable to the Lord, as in days gone by, as in former years" (Mal. 3:3-4).

God had indicted the priests (spiritual leaders) for their failure to worship correctly and reminded them of the effect this was having on His people: "For the lips of a priest ought to preserve knowledge, and from his mouth men should seek instruction—because he is the messenger of the Lord Almighty. But you have turned from the way and by your teaching have caused many to stumble" (Mal 2:7-8).

The apostle Paul was so aware of the affect of his relationship with God (daily and deep worship), that he pled with the spiritual leaders in Ephesus to give great care to their lives: "Therefore, I declare to you today that I am innocent of the blood of all men. For I have not hesitated to proclaim to you the whole will of God. Keep watch over yourselves and all the flock of which the Holy Spirit has made you overseers. Be shepherds of the church of God, which he bought with his own blood. I know that after I leave, savage wolves will come in among you and will not spare the flock. Even from your own number

But who can endure the day of his coming? Who can stand when he appears? For he will be like a refiner's fire or a launderer's soap. He will sit as a refiner and a purifier of silver; he will purify the Levites and refine them like gold and silver. Then the Lord will have men who will bring offerings in righteousness, and the offerings of Judah and Jerusalem will be acceptable to the Lord, as in days gone by, as in former years.

— Malachi 3:2-4

men will arise and distort the truth in order to draw away disciples after them. So be on your guard! Remember that for three years I never stopped warning each of you night and day with tears. Now I commit you to God and to the word of his grace, which can build you up and give you an inheritance among all those who are sanctified" (Acts 20:26-32).

Throughout the Scripture God constantly reviews the quality of worship of the spiritual leaders of His people: the king, the princes, the priests, and the prophets (Jer. 4:9; 5:30-31).

Other spiritual leaders that will encourage you and greatly instruct you include:

- Daniel (Dan. 9)
- Aaron—who did not "restrain the people," and let them sin to their shame among their enemies (Ex. 32:25)
- The faithful priests of Ezekiel's time (Ezek. 44:15-16,23)

If God and men consider you a spiritual leader, how are you serving faithfully, especially in your worship?

_____

_____

Are you willing to accept the spiritual responsibility for the condition of the worship of God's people under your care?

_____

How?

_____

If you are a father or a mother, how are you being a spiritual leader who is positively affecting your family?

_____

When you worship, in what ways are others greatly encouraged to worship also?

_____

_____

"But the priests, who are Levites and descendants of Zadok and who faithfully carried out the duties of my sanctuary when the Israelites went astray from me, are to come near to minister before me; they are to stand before me to offer sacrifices of fat and blood, declares the Sovereign Lord. They alone are to enter my sanctuary; they alone are to come near my table to minister before me and perform my service."

— Ezekiel 44:15-16

Heaven's Pattern for Worship

At the beginning of the fourth chapter of the Book of Revelation, we find that a door to heaven has been opened to the apostle John. "After these things I looked, and behold, a door standing open in heaven" (Rev. 4:1, NASB). As he looks through this door, he witnesses the continuous, perfect worship of heaven itself. He describes in intricate detail what he sees taking place. And what a contrast it is to what is taking place on earth, as has been described in the previous two chapters.

In chapters 2 and 3, the Lord Jesus dictates seven letters to John, letters John was to make sure were delivered to seven churches on the mainland, churches that were not too far from where John was exiled on the island of Patmos. To five of these churches the Lord issued a severe warning. In each letter He exposed areas where the church needed to repent and make corrections, and if the churches did not heed the warning, the Lord said He would remove His presence from them.

One of these churches had the reputation of being "alive," but Jesus said it was dead. Another church was considered to be "rich," having a lot of money, but Jesus said that it was poor. These churches were part of the early church that just a few years before had been turning the world upside down. John, one of the apostles who had walked with Jesus, was still living, but already these churches were beginning to turn their hearts away from God, just as the children of Israel had done so often under the Old Covenant.

Read Revelation 2:4, 14, and 20. Each of these verses follows a commendation of God to a congregation. Then, God addresses fault that He has found in otherwise exemplary churches. Is it possible that we today might be thinking that we are doing just fine, while the Lord has a different opinion of us? Is it possible that, even though your congregation

Key Verse

You are worthy, our Lord and God, to receive glory and honor and power, for you created all things, and by your will they were created and have their being.

— Revelation 4:11

This Week's Lessons

1. Worship and the Glory of God

2. Worship and the Authority of God

3. The Eternity of God and How It Affects Us

4. Worship and the Activity of God in History

5. Why Is My Response So Important to God?

Worship is the adoring response of the creature to the infinite majesty of God. While it presupposes submission to Him, to worship, in the highest sense, is not supplication for needs, or even thanksgiving for blessings, but the occupation of the soul with God Himself. . . . The end of it all is the pure joy of magnifying the One who alone is worthy.

— Robert E. Coleman

"Yet I hold this against you: You have forsaken your first love. . . . Nevertheless, I have a few things against you: You have people there who hold to the teaching of Balaam, who taught Balak to entice the Israelites to sin by eating food sacrificed to idols and by committing sexual immorality. . . . Nevertheless, I have this against you: You tolerate that woman Jezebel, who calls herself a prophetess. By her teaching she misleads my servants into sexual immorality and the eating of food sacrificed to idols."

— Revelation 2:4, 14, 20

has a certain reputation, the Lord may see things differently? Reflect on your congregation. What do you think God sees?

_____

_____

_____

As we look this week at the worship that is taking place in heaven and place God's standard against our own lives and churches, may we be ready and willing to hear what the Holy Spirit is saying to us, the church today, and be quick to make the necessary adjustments to bring ourselves in line with God's Word.

This week's text is Revelation 4:1-11. Read it each day this week.

Day 1: Worship and the Glory of God

Have you ever considered how important God's "glory" is in worship? There are many references to it in both the Old and New Testaments. In today's study we will look at two aspects of God's glory:

1. The glory of God's "presence" in worship.
2. The glory God is due in worship.

The Glory of God's Presence

In 2 Chronicles 7:1-3, immediately following Solomon's prayer of dedication for the Temple, we read; "Fire came down from heaven and consumed the burnt offering and the sacrifices, and the glory of the Lord filled the temple. The priests could not enter the temple of the Lord because the glory of the Lord filled it. When all the Israelites saw the fire coming down and the glory of the Lord on the temple, they knelt on the pavement with their faces to the ground, and they worshiped and gave thanks to the Lord."

The "glory of the Lord" here, simply stated, is the "manifest presence of the Lord." His glory is where He reveals or manifests Himself. The "glory of God" is the revelation and manifestation of our Lord's nature and being. The Lord's response to Solomon's prayer was to appear in an awesome demonstration of His holiness and power. He revealed Himself in fire, and it was so overwhelming that the priests dared not even enter the temple. Wherever God is, there is fire. In Deuteronomy 4:24, God is described like this: "For the Lord your God is a consuming fire, a jealous God." The writer to the Hebrews also records those very words: "For our 'God is a consuming fire'" (Heb. 12:29).

Fire was the evidence of God's glory and presence for Moses when he met God on Mt. Sinai. "To the Israelites the glory of the Lord looked like a consuming fire on top of the mountain" (Ex. 24:17). This was so when Elijah faced the prophets of Baal. "Then the fire of the Lord fell and burned up the sacrifice" (1 Kings 18:38). The sacrifice, the worship that Elijah was offering, was authenticated by God by His coming in fire.

It was so in Isaiah's worship encounter with God in the sixth chapter of his book. Isaiah saw the glory of God and was overcome with his own sinfulness. Upon confession of his sin, the seraph took a coal from the burning altar and applied it to the point of Isaiah's confession, and he was forgiven and cleansed. The altar represents Calvary, and the coal represents the blood of our Savior. The Gospel writer John, in referring to Isaiah's worship encounter said, "Isaiah said this because he saw Jesus' glory and spoke about him" (John 12:41).

The "glory of the Lord" is the "manifest presence of the Lord." His glory is where He reveals or manifests Himself.

Now let's look at what fire does. When we think of fire, we are prone to think only of the dramatic and spectacular. It can be that, but it is much more. Fire gives light; fire warms; it purifies, melts, heats, cleanses, and consumes. Fire also produces power when correctly harnessed and channeled. How did God make His presence known on the Day of Pentecost? Tongues of fire descended upon the worshiping followers of Christ in the upper room. Immediately after God had manifested His glory in this way, they went forth into the world, in power, to turn their world upside down.

Read John 12:37-41, which quotes from Isaiah 53:1 and 6:10. Could the reason for the powerlessness of so much of the church today be because the glory of God may not be present in our worship? Has any part of your life been consumed or cleansed by the cleansing presence of God? Explain.

_____

_____

_____

Wherever genuine worship is taking place, the fire of God will be at work. Though it is unlikely that it will be as dramatic as the instances mentioned above, there will be evidences of the fire's presence. Oh that that would always be true in all our churches for without the glory of God, without the presence of God, without the fire of God, worship is as useless as an empty fireplace on a cold winter night. We can dance and make a lot of noise, and we can work up emotions and create good feelings, but if there is never any sense of the glory, the holiness, the awesomeness of God in our worship, we will end up unchanged. There will be no transformation. If there is no fire, there will be no light to show us our sinfulness. Without light there is no conviction of sin, thus no repentance. Without repentance there is no forgiveness and cleansing. Without forgiveness and cleansing there is no power for living and witness.

Blaise Paschal, a famous 17th-century French scientist, who, to this day, is considered to be one of the world's greatest minds, had a personal encounter with the glory of God one night that literally changed his life forever. He wrote about this experience on a piece of paper that he carried in a pocket next to his heart until he died. Those attending him on his deathbed found the paper, and in Paschal's personal handwriting read: "From about ten-thirty last night to about twelve-thirty this morning, FIRE! O Great God of Abraham, Isaac, and Jacob. Not the god of the philosophers and the wise, but the God of Jesus Christ who can only be known through His gospel. Security, feeling, peace, tears of joy. Amen!" Following the experience that prompted the writing of these words, Paschal went on to become one of the most powerful witnesses for Christ that the nation of France has ever known.

Are you experiencing the glory of God in your personal and corporate worship? That is not to say that everyone is going to have a "Paschal" experience or an "Isaiah" encounter; nor will our worship *always* be accompanied by an extraordinary sense of God's presence. There should, however, always be the consciousness that we are worshiping a holy, awesome, powerful God, who, at any time, might choose to reveal Himself in a special manifestation of His glory. Describe the level of consciousness of God's presence present in your worship.

_____

_____

_____

In the fourth chapter of Revelation, the apostle John was overwhelmed at the sight he saw when he looked through that open door into heaven and witnessed the glory of God. It is God's will that we, too, through the work of the Holy Spirit, our Teacher and Enabler, be overwhelmed with God's glory as we continuously grow in our knowledge and understanding of Him whom we worship. And the exciting thing is, as we do, we individually, and as a church, "with unveiled faces all reflect the Lord's glory, are being transformed into his likeness with ever-increasing glory, which comes from the Lord, who is the Spirit" (2 Cor. 3:18).

Transformed into the same image from glory to glory! Should that not be the goal of every worship leader, to see the church transformed into the same image of Christ? Should that not be the desire of all worshipers, to let Christ be formed in them? Ask God to show you whether this work of grace is taking place in your life.

The Glory God Is Due in Worship

Many references in Scripture remind us that God is the only One who is worthy of worship. He makes clear that no glory is to go to any other.

Transformed into the same image from glory to glory! Should that not be the goal of every worship leader, to see the church transformed into the same image of Christ? Should that not be the desire of all worshipers, to let Christ be formed in them? Ask God to show you whether this work of grace is taking place in your life.

"I am the Lord; that is my name! I will not give my glory to another" (Isa. 42:8). "Ascribe to the Lord glory and strength, ascribe to the Lord the glory due his name. Bring an offering and come before him; worship the Lord in the splendor of his holiness!" (1 Chron. 16:28-29).

God will not share His glory with anyone. "I am the Lord; that is my name! I will not give my glory to another" (Isa. 42:8). We cannot take for ourselves the glory that belongs to God alone and expect our worship to be acceptable to Him. In the context of worship today, however, especially in the area of music, where it is so easy to concentrate on performing rather than on ministering in the Spirit of God and leading people to focus on the Lord, there is a danger that people will become more impressed with the vehicle, with the instrument, with the talent, than with God.

What a tragedy it is when God is used to display man's talent rather than man's talent being used to display God. The same can be true in preaching or in any other area of service. For true worship to take place, God who must be on center stage. This is something that every believer must take to heart and continuously remember.

While ministering in Toronto, Canada, many years ago, a woman gave me (Ron) a poem she had just written. This poem, "Touch Not the Glory," expresses so well the need we all have of being careful that, in whatever we are doing, God alone gets the glory:

> Should God call you to serve where others tried and failed,
> But with God's help and strength your efforts will prevail;
> Touch not the glory!
>
> Have you some special gift, some riches you can share?
> Or are you called of God to intercessory prayer?
> Touch not the glory!
>
> Has God appointed you to some great noble cause?
> Or put you where you hear the sound of man's applause?
> Touch not the glory!
>
> A watching world still waits to see what can be done
> Through one who touches not that which is God's alone.
> Touch not the glory, for it belongs to God!
>
> —Erma Davidson/© 1993 Ron & Patricia Owens

It matters not if the world has heard or approves or understands. The only applause we're meant to seek is the applause of nail-scarred hands.

We cannot take for ourselves the glory that belongs to God alone and expect our worship to be acceptable to Him.

The psalmist said: "Ascribe to the Lord the glory due his name; bring an offering and come into his courts. Worship the Lord in the splendor of his holiness; tremble before him, all the earth" (Ps. 96:8-9).

The apostle John said: "Then I heard every creature in heaven and on earth and under the earth and on the sea, and all that is in them, singing: 'To him who sits on the throne and to the Lamb be praise and honor and glory and power, for ever and ever!' The four living creatures said, 'Amen,' and the elders fell down and worshiped" (Rev. 5:13-14).

Day 2: Worship and the Authority of God

My wife and I (Ron) were recently in a restaurant in Florida. A young waiter came to see what we wanted to drink, and when we told him that we just wanted water and lemon, his reply was, "Awesome!" I looked at my wife and said: "Awesome? What's awesome about that?" I realize that he was just throwing a word around that was void of any true meaning to him, yet this incident serves as an example of how far removed we can get from the true reality of things.

We may react to the trite use of such a word to describe a water and lemon drink order, but is that really much different from believers who live with little or no sense of awe and wonder toward the things of God, seldom if ever impressed with the grandeur and majesty of the Creator?

In the fourth chapter of Revelation, the apostle John was overwhelmed with the sight of the throne of God. He mentions it 10 times in this one chapter. Read Revelation 4:9-11. What comes to mind when you think of a throne? What does a throne represent?

_____

_____

_____

A throne represents sovereignty and authority. A throne is what a ruler, a king, sits on. When we come to worship, we are coming to a throne upon which sits the Sovereign God of the universe. When we worship, we acknowledge that all authority, power, dominion, control, and supremacy belong to Him. This was the throne Isaiah saw. It was the same throne Ezekiel saw in his first vision. "Above the expanse over their heads was what looked like a throne of sapphire, and high above on the throne was a figure like that of a man . . . and brilliant light surrounded him. . . . This was the appearance of the likeness of the glory of the Lord. When I saw it, I fell facedown" (Ezek. 1:26-28).

The God we worship is the One who has absolute authority and complete sovereignty over all things, includes you and me. Nothing ever happens that is beyond His control. Jesus said that not even a sparrow falls to the ground apart from the Father's will (Matt. 10:29). If we were really to grasp this, what a difference it would make in daily living, in our reactions to life.

Whenever the living creatures give glory, honor and thanks to him who sits on the throne and who lives for ever and ever, the twenty-four elders fall down before him who sits on the throne, and worship him who lives for ever and ever. They lay their crowns before the throne and say:

"You are worthy, our Lord and God, to receive glory and honor and power, for you created all things, and by your will they were created and have their being."

— Revelation 4:9-11

96

When true worship is taking place, we see God as the God whose throne is above the world. We see Him as the God who lives outside of time. We see Him as Moses saw Him: "Lord, you have been our dwelling place throughout all generations. Before the mountains were born or you brought forth the earth and the world, from everlasting to everlasting you are God" (Ps. 90:1-2).

Now let's contrast the God Moses knew with the gods Israel had begun to worship in Isaiah's day. They had begun to worship the gods of the nations around them, and these gods had to be carried or pulled on a cart. After all that God had done for them, they had turned to idols of their own making. God was grieved and reminded them of all the times He had carried them. He had carried them from the womb until old age, and not once had they ever had to carry Him (Isa. 46:1-7).

Let's look at how this can apply to us today. We may not be pulling actual wooden or stone gods on a cart, but our view of the God we worship may be such that we feel He is not quite up to meeting our needs. He is not strong enough to carry us through a given situation. How this inadequate view of Himself grieves the Lord!

Do we worship gods of wood and stone today? Some do. Their god is something they have created, built, or bought. Rather than their life being hidden in, and existing in, God, it consists of outward man-made creations that have to be "carried." The moment something happens to these creations, their world starts falling apart.

Think of God as sovereign, powerful, and with authority over all creation. How does thinking of God this way affect your worship?

_____

_____

Think of God as able to carry you through any circumstance—good times and bad. Does this change your attitude in worship? In what way?

_____

_____

Sometimes the things that we think of as necessary to carry us (money, possessions, influence, power, occupation) are actually things we must carry. We may spend so much time on these things that we have made

When true worship is taking place, we see God as the God whose throne is above the world. We see Him as the God who lives outside of time.

When we come to worship, we come to acknowledge the authority and sovereignty of God. He is from everlasting to everlasting, to whom all blessing, honor, glory, and power are due!

them into items of worship. What are you carrying in your life to the point of worshiping it? How can you change the focus of your worship from this man-made idol to the Sovereign God of the universe?

_____

_____

_____

How does knowing that God is capable carry you through all circumstances?

_____

_____

How often we worship a lesser God than our God really is. God never has and never will need a support system. Our God does not need to be carried on a cart. He is from everlasting to everlasting. When we gather to worship, this is the God before whom we bow. The psalmist was convinced of this when he wrote: "Blessed is he whose help is the God of Jacob, whose hope is in the Lord his God, the Maker of heaven and earth, the sea, and everything in them—the Lord, who remains faithful forever. He upholds the cause of the oppressed and gives food to the hungry. The Lord sets prisoners free. . . . The Lord reigns forever, your God, O Zion, for all generations. Praise the Lord" (Ps. 146:5-7, 10).

We must never forget that when we gather to worship we are coming to a throne. This is where worship begins. This is what dominated John's mind as he wrote down what he was seeing in heaven—the throne, the throne upon which sits the Supreme Sovereign of the universe, the One who has absolute authority over our lives, the One who has absolute authority over the universe. When we come to worship, we come to acknowledge the authority and sovereignty of God. He is from everlasting to everlasting, to whom all blessing, honor, glory, and power are due! Amen!

Day 3: The Eternity of God and How It Affects Us

It is impossible for the human mind to understand the things of God. We come to a study, such as worship, and the study of the eternity of God in particular, utterly dependent on God to help us grasp something of the magnitude of who He is. And who we see Him to be will be directly reflected in how we approach Him in worship. We are encouraged, however, in knowing that we have living in us the One whom our Lord asked the Father to send, the Holy Spirit, to guide and to teach us.

Over and over in Revelation we read, "who lives for ever and ever." The God we worship is the God who lives forever. When Moses asked God who he should say had sent him, "God said to Moses, 'I AM WHO I AM. This is what you are to say to the Israelites: "I AM has sent me to you"'"(Ex. 3:14). He is the One who lives in the ever present, with no beginning or ending.

Years later, Moses, looking back over the journey he and the children of Israel had made with the One whose name is I AM, prays: "Lord, you have been our dwelling place throughout all generations. Before the mountains were born or you brought forth the earth and the world, from everlasting to everlasting you are God. . . . For a thousand years in your sight are like a day that has just gone by, or like a watch in the night" (Ps. 90:1-2,4).

Read the definition of *worship* in the sidebar. One of the things the definition refers to is "the occupation of the soul with God Himself." Explain in your own words what it means for the soul to be "occupied" with God.

_____

_____

_____

Moses also addressed the brevity and frailty of man's life, but before he does, he reminds them of the awesome "I AM" who is their home, the One in whom and by whom, they live. And the One we worship is the same One of whom Moses spoke. God's care for His children is not confined to one generation or to a certain age group; it is forever, for all His children.

> Each of the four living creatures had six wings and was covered with eyes all around, even under his wings. Day and night they never stop saying: "Holy, holy, holy is the Lord God Almighty, who was, and is, and is to come."
>
> — Revelation 4:8

> *Worship is the adoring response of the creature to the infinite majesty of God. While it presupposes submission to Him, to worship, in the highest sense, is not supplication for needs, or even thanksgiving for blessings, but the occupation of the soul with God Himself. . . . The end of it all is the pure joy of magnifying the One who alone is worthy.*
>
> — Robert E. Coleman

Just as God is eternal in His very essence, meaning that everything He does He does from an eternal perspective, so it is with us, eternal beings; every thing we do has eternal consequences. No one lives for time alone.

Moses describes the eternity of God, His everlastingness, as preceding the creation of the world—"before the mountains were born or you brought forth the earth and the world." The world has a point of beginning. God doesn't. The world once was nothing. God always is. The eternity of God is the foundation of everything else God is, and it begins with His name which itself, is eternal. "I AM" describes one with no past and no future. He is the only one who can be called by that name. No other gods or founders of religions can claim that name.

Unlike God, however, His creatures are always in constant change. Every day our bodies, our perceptions, our plans, our lives, are changing. What we were this morning we will not be tonight because we will be one day closer to the end of our earthly lives than when we awoke. And we can never return to what we were this morning. We can't go back. We can never recoup the past. God, however, always *is*. He doesn't have a past to recoup.

How does God's eternity affect people in general? It affects them in many ways, but let's look at one fundamental way. Our Father is eternal, and therefore, all are eternal. Not in the broadest meaning of that word, because we had a beginning, but in the sense that man, created in the image of God, will live forever, whether with Him in heaven, or separated from Him in hell. And just as God is eternal in His very essence, meaning that everything He does He does from an eternal perspective, so it is with us, eternal beings; every thing we do has eternal consequences. No one lives for time alone.

How does God's eternity affect Christians? We are God's new creation (2 Cor. 5:17), and His covenant relationship with us is not a short-term experiment. It is for eternity. Some believers, however, though knowing this in their heads, live as though they were accountable for time alone. They live with little sense of being eternal and that their actions will have eternal consequences. Many live for the moment, not thinking how that moment can, and will, affect their future.

All of us, I expect, if we could go back, would do some things differently. There are choices, that if given the opportunity, we would like to make over. We can't go back, however, because those actions are forever sealed in the past. But should that cause us to despair? Absolutely not! Because this great I AM, our Father, so loved us that He made every provision we need to be free of the past and the guilt to which Satan would love to keep us bound. Though there are consequences and sometimes scars for past actions, and things may never be quite the same again, we can be free from any bondage to the past forever—for eternity! And this, of course, is also true for those who have yet to come to Christ, no matter how great the sin, the blood of Christ can cleanse them from all sin.

What are you free to do since Christ has freed you from the past and guilt? Are you free to forgive? free to trust? free to love? Explain your answers.

_____

_____

_____

The wonder of repentance and forgiveness is that our yesterdays can be erased, blotted out, and thrown into the sea of God's forgetfulness (Ps. 103:12; Jer. 31:34). Oh how thankful we ought to be that we who are eternal beings don't have to live forever with the mistakes or the transgressions of the past, because, right in the middle of our eternity stands the cross!

> The cross is that point in history where eternity merges with time.
> The guilt of a world meets the Savior, the sins that He carried were mine.
> Through the blood of my blessed Redeemer I have been reinstated with Him;
> The past is forgotten and buried, for God has forgiven my sin.
>
> No longer can Satan accuse me, when he does it is nothing but lies.
> I tell him with each accusation, the blood of my Savior applies.
> Not only for now but forever, I am sealed by the blood shed that day—
> Forever, forever, forever, hallelujah thank God I can say:
> I'm forgiven!
>
> —Ron Owens/© 1989 Ron & Patricia Owens

If God is eternal, then the Lord Jesus is eternal. It is interesting to note that in Isaiah 9:6, the prophet prophecies that one of the names our Lord would be called is "Everlasting Father." Jesus was the fleshing out of the Eternal Father here on earth. He was the complete revelation

Oh how thankful we ought to be that we who are eternal beings don't have to live forever with the mistakes or the transgressions of the past, because, right in the middle of our eternity stands the cross!

of the Father, so much so that Jesus said in John 14:9, "Anyone who has seen me has seen the Father."

Jesus spoke of His eternity with the Father when He said, "I came from the Father and entered the world; now I am leaving the world and going back to the Father" (John 16:28). In John 17:5, Jesus prayed: "And now, Father, glorify me in your presence with the glory I had with you before the world began."

The writer to the Hebrews said: "Jesus Christ is the same yesterday [eternity past] and today [eternity present] and forever [eternity future]" (Heb. 13:8). We read in Ephesians 3:11 that all is "according to his eternal purpose which he accomplished in Christ Jesus our Lord."

When we worship, we acknowledge that there was a time when we were not, but there never was a time when He was not. God does not exist in time; time exists in God. God does not exist in space; space exists in God. We worship the One for whom a thousand years is as a day, the One who is not bound by watches and calendars. The apostle Paul put it this way: "For since the creation of the world God's invisible qualities—his eternal power and divine nature—have been clearly seen" (Rom. 1:20).

Read Romans 1:20 and ponder what it means to know that God's eternal power impacts this very moment and can do so with eternal results. Yet, compared to eternity, this hour is less than a molecule floating in space. Describe how that affects your perspective on God's nature and His attention to us.

_____

_____

_____

When we worship, we acknowledge the foreverness of God! We proclaim the eternity of the One who sits on the throne (Rev. 5:13). If then, God is eternal, He is worthy of our deepest love and our most profound adoration and thanksgiving. If God is eternal, He is worthy of our never-ending service, obedience, and devotion. He is eternal! Let's offer Him the worship He is due.

For since the creation of the world God's invisible qualities—his eternal power and divine nature—have been clearly seen, being understood from what has been made, so that men are without excuse.

— Romans 1:20

Additional Scriptures on the Eternity of God

Eternal God

Deuteronomy 33:27: "The eternal God is your refuge, and underneath are the everlasting arms."

1 Timothy 1:17: "Now to the King eternal, immortal, invisible, the only God, be honor and glory for ever and ever."

Eternal Life

John 3:15: "Everyone who believes in him may have eternal life."

John 4:14: "Whoever drinks the water I give him will never thirst. Indeed, the water I give him will become in him a spring of water welling up to eternal life."

Romans 6:23: "For the wages of sin is death, but the gift of God is eternal life in Christ Jesus our Lord."

1 John 5:11,13: "And this is the testimony: God has given us eternal life, and this life is in his Son. . . . I write these things to you who believe in the name of the Son of God so that you may know that you have eternal life."

John 6:68: "Simon Peter answered him, 'Lord, to whom shall we go? You have the words of eternal life.'"

John 10:28: "I give them eternal life, and they shall never perish; no one can snatch them out of my hand."

John 17:3: "Now this is eternal life: that they may know you, the only true God, and Jesus Christ, whom you have sent."

Eternal Joy and Pleasure

Psalm 16:11: "You have made known to me the path of life; you will fill me with joy in your presence, with eternal pleasures at your right hand."

Eternal Praise

Psalm 111:10: "The fear of the Lord is the beginning of wisdom. . . . To him belongs eternal praise."

Eternal Punishment

Matthew 25:46: "Then they will go away to eternal punishment, but the righteous to eternal life."

Eternal Glory

2 Corinthians 4:17: "For our light and momentary troubles are achieving for us an eternal glory that far outweighs them all."

Eternal Redemption

Hebrews 9:12: "He did not enter by means of the blood of goats and calves; but he entered the Most Holy Place once for all by his own blood, having obtained eternal redemption."

Eternal Word

1 Peter 1:25: "But the word of the Lord stands forever."

Eternal Savior

Hebrews 13:8: "Jesus Christ is the same yesterday and today and forever."

Eternity

Ecclesiastes 3:11: "He has made everything beautiful in its time. He has also set eternity in the hearts of men; yet they cannot fathom what God has done from beginning to end."

Eternal Throne

Hebrews 1:8: "Your throne, O God, will last for ever and ever."

Eternal Beginning and Ending

Revelation 22:13: "I am the Alpha and the Omega, the First and the Last, the Beginning and the End."

After reading this list of Scriptures, collect some of your thoughts about God that the verses have inspired and write them here.

_____

_____

_____

Day 4: Worship and the Activity of God in History

Today read Revelation 4:11 through chapter 5.

Yesterday we considered the eternity of God and how it affects each of us. Today we are looking at the activity of God in history. But how do we begin even to touch such a vast subject as this in such a brief time. We again must depend totally on the Holy Spirit to help us expand our understanding of the magnitude of God's works. For some it hopefully may be the beginning of a further study you will personally make.

Here in this passage we observe that, in the worship of heaven, the worshipers are acknowledging the activity of God in creation. "You are worthy, our Lord and God, to receive glory and honor and power, for you created all things, and by your will they were created and have their being" (Rev. 4:11).

When we worship here on earth, we too are acknowledging God's activity in creation. He is the One by whose hand we were created. The one who masterfully put together these bodies of ours that contain approximately 10 trillion cells, each cell containing at least 100,000 genes that make up our own personal genetic code that is unique from every other human being who ever lived—past, present, or future. And every minute approximately three billion of our cells die, and every minute three billion new cells are formed to replace the old ones, each cell containing the 100,000 genes. To think how many times this is done on a daily basis is incredible.

He is the One by whom the universe was formed. Scientists now tell us that in the "known" universe that there are more than 100 billion galaxies, each one containing at least 100 billion stars. He is the One of whom Job said: "And these are but the outer fringe of his works; how faint the whisper we hear of him! Who then can understand the thunder of his power?" (Job 26:14; also see Job 38:4-6).

Job knew that before we can really understand the activity of God we must understand His ways, His power, and the power behind all that He does. That was the basic difference between Moses' understanding of God and that of the children of Israel; Moses knew God's ways, while the people understood only His acts (Ps. 103:7). But Job says, "Who can understand" these things? Job is asking, who has the capacity to comprehend the power of God? His power cannot be compared to the greatest power man has created. Man thinks in terms of what he can see and understand. He relates to what happens here on earth. He brags about the energy produced through nuclear fission. He marvels at the force of jet propulsion. But what are these compared to the power of God? We observe small displays of it in thunder and lightening. We may briefly tremble at the force of hurricane and tornado-like winds. But what are even these compared to the power of God?

Let's look at one example of the awesomeness of God's power that profoundly impacted me (Ron) several years ago. I read how in one of those 100 billion plus galaxies that man has been able to determine are "out there," they recently discovered the largest black hole known to exist in space. It is 50 million light years from where we are. Light travels at almost 6 trillion miles a year, so you multiply one by the other and you get the mileage. Just one one-way trip in a compact car would seriously deplete the oil and gas reserves of our planet. That, by the way, is not far in terms of some of the distances in space.

But it wasn't the distance that caught my attention, it was the density of that black hole, from which no light can escape. They compared the density to the compacting of planet Earth down to the size of a marble. All the continents, everything, down to something you could hold in your hand. When I read that, my first thought was, "He's got the whole world in His hand!" Then suddenly I realized that I had lost the wonder of this God of creation. It had been a long time since I had stopped to consider the greatness of God in His creation. In the busyness of ministry, I had lost the awe and wonder of the magnitude of the God I serve.

Have you lost the wonder of God in creation? Read Psalm 139:13-14. Recall that you, too, are part of God's magnificent creation. Which is most incredible to you: that God created the billions of stars or that God created and cares for you personally? Write a prayer thanking God for His creation.

_____

_____

_____

_____

Why is it that the more we know about God's creation, the less in awe we are of the Creator? The psalmist did not know a fraction of what we know, yet, when he looked at the night skies, from deep

> For you created my inmost being; you knit me together in my mother's womb. I praise you because I am fearfully and wonderfully made; your works are wonderful, I know that full well.
>
> — Psalm 139:13-14

within the heart of one who was a true worshiper, he exclaimed, "The heavens declare the glory of God; the skies proclaim the work of his hands. Day after day they pour forth speech; night after night they display knowledge" (Ps. 19:1-2). Can we really offer God the worship He deserves if we no longer "wonder," if we no longer stand in awe of what He has done? Have you lost the wonder? Is your worship motivated at all by the greatness of the God of creation?

Not only does John hear heavenly creatures acknowledging the activity of God in creation; he also observes them acknowledging the activity of God in redemption. He sees a lamb! "Then I saw a Lamb, looking as if it had been slain, standing in the center of the throne, encircled by the four living creatures and the elders. He had seven horns and seven eyes, which are the seven spirits of God sent out into all the earth. . . . And they sang a new song: 'You are worthy to take the scroll and to open its seals, because you were slain, and with your blood you purchased men for God from every tribe and language and people and nation'" (Rev. 5:6,9).

The loudest hallelujahs, the greatest crescendos of praise and adoration are reserved for the activity of God in redemption. They are worshiping a lamb, the Lamb of redemption. That same God who created all things, who flung those 100 billion galaxies into space is the same God who came to earth, hung on a cross, and died for you and me. The greatest tragedy of all is when those who claim to worship God have lost the wonder and awe of the God of redemption.

When we gather to worship, we are worshiping the God of creation. When we gather to worship, we are worshiping the God of redemption. How often, however, have we sung of the awesomeness of God in His redemptive activity without being so moved in our inner being that we had to cry out, as did David, in declaring the magnitude of the God we worship? O God, how great You are! Forgive us for worshiping a lesser God than You are.

If the awe of who God is has been lost, what can be done to restore it? The beginning point is to turn to God's Word where He describes Himself in all His greatness.

Listen to the psalmist. "For the Lord is the great God, the great King above all gods. In his hand are the depths of the earth, and the mountain peaks belong to him. The sea is his, for he made it, and his hands formed the dry land. Come, let us bow down in worship, let us kneel before the Lord our Maker; for he is our God and we are the people of his pasture, the flock under his care" (Ps. 95:3-7). "How awesome is the Lord Most High, the great King over all the earth!" (Ps. 47:2).

"Worthy is the Lamb, who was slain, to receive power and wealth and wisdom and strength and honor and glory and praise!"

— Revelation 5:12

Whenever the living creatures give glory, honor and thanks to him who sits on the throne and who lives for ever and ever, the twenty-four elders fall down before him who sits on the throne, and worship him who lives for ever and ever. They lay their crowns before the throne.

— Revelation 4:9-10

Day 5: Why Is My Response So Important to God?

From what we observe in the worship of heaven, worship does not stop with the proclaiming of God's greatness, His holiness, and His awesome activity in creation and redemption, but we find the hosts of heaven "responding" to the One on the throne. Worship is incomplete without response to the One we are worshiping.

It is one thing to declare that God is worthy of all these things, but it is another thing to do what we find them doing in heaven, responding to the One whose greatness they are declaring.

Our Response in Worship: In Submission

There seems to be no question in the hearts of those who are worshiping in heaven as to what their response must be to the One seated on the throne. We find them putting feet to their proclaiming of His greatness by submitting themselves to the One they are worshiping. There is no true worship without submission.

It is one thing to acknowledge the authority, eternity, and activity of God in creation and redemption, but it is quite another to respond and submit to that authority in a way that shows we really believe what we are saying. This is what Jesus was pointing out to His disciples in John 14:15 when He said, "If you love me, you will obey what I command." In other words, "you will prove to me that you really mean what you are saying to me by doing what I ask you to do."

It is often uncomfortable to place what we think and do against the standard of God's Word. We sometimes quick to make excuses and to try to justify our way of thinking, but this does not change what God says. But when the Holy Spirit, our Teacher, convicts of sin, of falling short of God's standards, and we respond to His call to a new depth of repentance and surrender, our eyes are then opened to His truth in a fresh way, and we can then make the adjustments, by His enabling, that bring joy to the One we worship. Remember what David said in Psalm 51:12? "Grant me a willing spirit, to sustain me." May that be our prayer.

Submission means to lay oneself flat in humility. We find the 24 elders doing this repeatedly in the worship scene of heaven. How can we respond in any other way than to stoop in submission before the One we worship if He really is who we say He is? Yet, is that the attitude and spirit of a lot of what is happening in the Christian world today?

In Isaiah 57:15, we read, "For this is what the high and lofty One says—he who lives forever, whose name is holy: 'I live in a high and holy place, but also with him who is contrite and lowly in spirit, to revive the spirit of the lowly and to revive the heart of the contrite.'"

In our Lord's Sermon on the Mount, He said, "Blessed are the poor in spirit [humble], for theirs is the kingdom of heaven" (Matt. 5:3). In Peter's first letter he said, "All of you, clothe yourselves with humility toward one another, because, 'God opposes the proud but gives grace to the humble'" (1 Pet. 5:5).

In what many believe to be God's formula for revival in 2 Chronicles 7:14, the humbling of self precedes everything else: "If my people, who are called by my name, will humble themselves and pray." Humbling of self even precedes the offering of prayers. The account of the publican and Pharisee praying in the temple reveals the heart attitude that God is looking for in our worship.

Humility is not seen as an admirable trait in the world today—even in ministry. Read again 2 Chronicles 7:14. Will God hear the prayers of church leaders who are not humble? How will you respond?

_____

_____

_____

The motto of the Welsh revival of 1904–05, when approximately one hundred thousand people were saved in a matter of six months, was "Bend the church and save the world!"

> Bend me lower, lower down at Jesus' feet,
> Holy Spirit, bend me 'till Your work's complete.
> Wash away the stain of sin, make me holy, pure within—
> Bend me lower down at Jesus' feet.
>
> —Ron Owens/© 1993 Ron & Patricia Owens

Our Response in Worship: In Abdication

"Whenever the living creatures give glory, honor and thanks to him who sits on the throne and who lives for ever and ever, the twenty-four elders fall down before him who sits on the throne, and worship him who lives for ever and ever. They lay their crowns before the throne" (Rev. 4:9-10).

One of the most sensitive issues in our society today is the matter of "rights." It has also become a major issue in the church. The matter of "rights" is at the heart of so many of our problems today. It is at the root of much of the breakup of the family unit. "I have my rights. I can

"If my people, who are called by my name, will humble themselves and pray and seek my face and turn from their wicked ways, then will I hear from heaven and will forgive their sin and will heal their land."

— 2 Chronicles 7:14

We sometimes forget what it cost our Lord to purchase our freedom. He gave up His "rights" to pay the debt of sin by dying on the cross.

do what I want to do." It is often at the root of church splits. Listen in on some church business meetings, and you hear the voice of the flesh demanding its rights, and if it doesn't get what it wants, it will pack its bag and leave, or it will stay put and cause problems until it gets its way.

We have gone so far in our land today—to give a mother the right to take the life of an unborn baby. And tragically this attitude is almost as great a problem in the church. Rights?

> My rights? Whose rights? God has bought me outright;
> I am no longer my own!
> My rights? Whose rights? God had bought me outright
> That through me His glory might be known.
> I belong to God, I am no longer my own.
>
> —Ron Owens/© 1993 Ron & Patricia Owens

We have let the world shape us into its mold in this matter. The apostle Paul reminded the believers in the church at Corinth that they had been bought with a price. We sometimes forget what it cost our Lord to purchase our freedom. He gave up His "rights" to pay the debt of sin by dying on the cross.

We are told to have this same mind that was in Christ, "Who, being in very nature God, did not consider equality with God something to be grasped, but made himself nothing, taking the very nature of a servant, being made in human likeness. And being found in appearance as a man, he humbled himself and became obedient to death—even death on a cross!" (Phil. 2:6-8).

God, the Lord of everything, became as nothing to die for us. When is the last time you sacrificed anything for anyone? What keeps you from being humble as Christ was humble? Do you need to sacrifice self for Christ? Write your commitment here.

_____

_____

_____

We see the 24 elders taking the crowns from off their own heads and laying them at the feet of the One they are worshiping. Crowns represent authority and rights, and in so doing they were saying that they were abdicating their rights to themselves and they were surrendering those rights to another, even to the One they were worshiping.

How can we apply that to ourselves, to the way we live and to our worship? We were bought with a price; we have given the rights to our lives to the One who purchased us with His blood; we are no longer our own. What difference would this make in the life of Christian families and in the life of our churches if we really believed this and lived our lives accordingly. What difference would this make in the way we approach God in our worship personally and corporately?

Now let's look at one last response. This is not a response we find in heaven because this particular response will have been completed when we are called home to worship in heaven. For this response we are going to go to Isaiah 6.

The Culmination or Climax of Worship

Though the church today places a good bit of emphasis on service, it is not often connected to worship. In reality it should be, because true service is worship, and there is no such thing as authentic worship without service. To put it another way, he who will not serve does not worship.

Worship is much more than many church members think it is. Though God can take delight in great congregational singing, well-prepared soloists and choirs, well-articulated prayers, and creative preaching, He will find no pleasure in any of this, nor will He receive what is offered to Him, if there is no intent on the part of the offerer to serve Him after the lights have been turned off and the doors of the church closed.

Many Christians act as though there is no connection between the way they live all week and what takes place in the Sunday morning worship service. They think that if they enjoy themselves, put something in the offering, etc. that God will surely be pleased, and that it doesn't matter what they do after they leave. After all, they have given Him an hour or so of "their" time. But it does matter to God.

The prophet Isaiah personifies the kind of worshiper God is seeking. The death of King Uzziah, to whom Isaiah was closely associated, had left a deep void in the young man's life. His friend, and cousin, the King had died, the earthly throne had lost its meaning, and now in his grief Isaiah turns to God. And as he turns to seek after God, he has a vision, and in his vision he sees another throne—the throne in heaven, the same one John saw. He saw seraphs, and he heard them calling out, one to the other: "Holy, holy, holy is the Lord Almighty; the whole earth is full of his glory" (Isa. 6:3).

Now notice the response Isaiah had to what he saw and heard. He was overcome by the awesome presence of God, and he cried out, "Woe

Though the church today places a good bit of emphasis on service, it is not often connected to worship. In reality it should be, because true service is worship, and there is no such thing as authentic worship without service. To put it another way, he who will not serve does not worship.

to me! . . . I am ruined! For I am a man of unclean lips, and I live among a people of unclean lips, and my eyes have seen the King, the Lord Almighty" (v. 5). Then immediately after this confession, one of the seraphs touched his lips with a red-hot coal from the altar, and his sin was cleansed.

At this point we observe one of the most thrilling things happen. Isaiah heard the Trinity speaking: "Whom shall I send? And who will go for us?" (v. 8). Then, echoing from one corner of the temple to the other, we hear the cry of a worshiping heart. We hear the response of one who has seen the Lord. We hear the words of one whose eyes and ears have been sensitized to the things of God. We hear the words of one who would never be the same again, who would forever be a worshiper of God alone. "Here am I. Send me!" (v. 8).

This is the response of one who has worshiped, who has seen the throne. The apostle Paul made this correlation for those in the church in Rome, and for us as well, when he said, "I urge you, brothers, in view of God's mercy, to offer your bodies as living sacrifices, holy and pleasing to God—this is your spiritual act of worship" (Rom. 12:1). True worship culminates, climaxes, and continues as we serve the One we worship. May our prayer be:

Take these hands, may they serve you in all they do;
Take this voice, may it speak day and night for you.
Take these feet, may they walk only in your ways,
Take my mind, eyes and ears, use them for your praise.

Lord, by your Spirit use me, may your light shine through me.
Lord, with your life refill me so the world around will see
Your hands extended to them, reaching for them,
You loving them through me, and show them Lord you died to set them free.
—Ron Owens/© 1986 Ron & Patricia Owens

This is the expression of a servant's heart, of one who has humbled himself, surrendered his rights, and is willing and ready to serve his Master at all costs. This is the life of a true worshiper.

What Would Happen if We Returned to Worship?

Not only does worship presuppose a relationship with God, but a true relationship presupposes that one is a worshiper. We were born to worship, and the living of the life of a worshiper begins in private. This is where the foundation of worship is laid; corporate worship is the public expression of what has been going on in a private relationship with the One we worship. I don't go to church to be a worshiper; I go to church because I am a worshiper. I go to church to join other worshipers in publicly worshiping the God I love.

In the Psalms, David said: "I rejoiced with those who said to me, 'Let us go to the house of the Lord'" (Ps. 122:1) He was not only ready to go; he was thrilled to go! He was eager to be a part of that gathering of saints who would be worshiping his Lord.

Why was David excited about "going to church?" Because he was a worshiper. There he would join his heart and voice in worship of the one true God. There he would experience something that happens only when believers are gathered together in corporate worship—the uniqueness of a corporate divine encounter with a holy God.

Do you think of worship in the way David did, with gladness? with the sense that was where he wanted to be? knew he belonged? longed to be there? Explain.

_____

_____

_____

_____

Key Verse
You also, like living stones, are being built into a spiritual house to be a royal priesthood, offering spiritual sacrifices acceptable to God through Jesus Christ.
— 1 Peter 2:5

This Week's Lessons
1. Here We Are, Send Us!
2. Worship and the Early Church
3. Why Christians Gather
4. Worship and Missions
5. Now It's Our Turn

Let us not give up meeting together, as some are in the habit of doing, but let us encourage one another—and all the more as you see the Day approaching.

— Hebrews 10:25

A great many of the "encounters with God while worshiping" were in corporate worship. A classic moment was recorded in 2 Chronicles 7:5-7. King Solomon led out, and all the people joined together. Solomon had built the temple and the ark of the covenant was being brought to the temple: "Then Solomon summoned to Jerusalem the elders of Israel, all the heads of the tribes and the chiefs of the Israelite families. . . . . All the men of Israel came together to the king. . . . King Solomon and the entire assembly of Israel that had gathered about him were before the ark. . . . The trumpeters and singers joined in unison, as with one voice, to give praise and thanks to the Lord. Accompanied by trumpets, cymbals and other instruments, they raised their voices in praise to the Lord and sang: 'He is good; his love endures forever.' Then the temple of the Lord was filled with a cloud, and the priests could not perform because of the cloud, for the glory of the Lord filled the temple of God" (2 Chron. 5:2-3,6,13-14).

This was followed by one of the great corporate prayers of the Bible, which was prayed according to the conditions of God's original covenant with the Hebrew people at Sinai. Then came these enormous words: "When Solomon finished praying, fire came down from heaven and consumed the burnt offering and the sacrifices, and the glory of the Lord filled the temple" (2 Chron. 7:1).

It is for this reason that God said through the writer of Hebrews: "Let us not give up meeting together, as some are in the habit of doing, but let us encourage one another—and all the more as you see the Day approaching" (Heb. 10:25).

From God's heart, He has so much He would reveal to His people, if they would return to Him. There is hardly a more plaintive cry from the loving heart of God for His people than that found in Ezekiel 18:30-32: "Repent! Turn away from all your offenses; then sin will not be your downfall. . . . Get a new heart. . . . Why will you die, O house of Israel? For I take no pleasure in the death of anyone. . . . Repent and live!"

Read Ezekiel 18:30-32. Underline what God instructs His people to do.
Circle God's reason for giving these instructions.
Summarize in a sentence what God feels for His people.

_____

_____

_____

_____

What would happen in our day, if God's people returned to true worship? This week we will explore this final, and crucial question about worship.

"Therefore, O house of Israel, I will judge you, each one according to his ways, declares the Sovereign Lord. Repent! Turn away from all your offenses; then sin will not be your downfall. Rid yourselves of all the offenses you have committed, and get a new heart and a new spirit. Why will you die, O house of Israel? For I take no pleasure in the death of anyone, declares the Sovereign Lord. Repent and live!"

— Ezekiel 18:30-32

Day 1: Here We Are, Send Us!

When God's people deliberately choose to stand before God in solemn worship, God sees, hears, and responds! The outcome is awesome. God, by His presence, "returns" and assures His people that He still has a significant assignment for them.

When the spiritual leaders, including the singers, consecrate themselves so they can lead God's people in worship (2 Chron. 5:11-14), everything is in place. As the worship proceeds—with singing, instruments, Scripture reading, prayer, and a message, God responds; and His presence fills the meeting place (2 Chron. 5:14; 7:1-3). Then the people worship and present themselves to the Lord and offer lavish offerings to God:

Read 2 Chronicles 7:3-4. Granted, the people had just seen fire come down from heaven, but do we not worship the same God? How much awe and reverence should we have for God? Describe what that would be like.

_____

_____

_____

But the worship of God's people had yet another dimension: their sacred place in the purposes of God to bless a nation, even to the ends of the earth. Hear carefully the invitation of God in 2 Chronicles 7:14-16: "If my people, who are called by my name, will humble themselves and pray and seek my face and turn from their wicked ways, then will I hear from heaven and will forgive their sin and will heal their land. Now my eyes will be open and my ears attentive to the prayers offered in this place. I have chosen and consecrated this temple so that my Name may be there forever. My eyes and my heart will always be there."

All God promised would be available to His people before a watching world. Such a corporate experience of God's people was God's pattern from the beginning. And His purpose was that both individuals, and all His people (a royal priesthood) would say, "Here we are, send us!"

So often God waits to give a loving and gracious assignment to His people, but they are not gathering in His presence with a heart to meet Him and hear Him. Hear God's heart for His people in Jeremiah's fateful day: "I spoke to you again and again, but you did not listen; I called

When all the Israelites saw the fire coming down and the glory of the Lord above the temple, they knelt on the pavement with their faces to the ground, and they worshiped and gave thanks to the Lord, saying, "He is good; his love endures forever." Then the king and all the people offered sacrifices before the Lord.

— 2 Chronicles 7:3-4

you, but you did not answer" (Jer. 7:13).

Just a little later He reminded them of His heart for His people: "From the time I brought your forefathers up from Egypt until today, I warned them again and again, saying, 'Obey me.' But they did not listen or pay attention; instead, they followed the stubbornness of their evil hearts. So I brought on them all the curses of the covenant I had commanded them to follow but that they did not keep'"(Jer. 11:7-8).

Read Malachi 3:10. What feeling do you think God expressed in the words He spoke to His people in this passage?

_____

_____

_____

What did God desire to give His people that they rejected?

_____

_____

_____

> "Test me in this," says the Lord Almighty, "and see if I will not throw open the floodgates of heaven and pour out so much blessing that you will not have room enough for it."
> — Malachi 3:10

Jesus expressed this same truth this way: "As the Father has loved me, so have I loved you. Now remain in my love. If you obey my commands, you will remain in my love, just as I have obeyed my Father's commands and remain in his love. I have told you this so that my joy may be in you and that your joy may be complete." (John 15:9-11).

The experiences of Isaiah as He worshiped God in the temple are so familiar to all of us (Isa. 6:1-8). This return of Isaiah to worship resulted in a revelation of God on His throne, a revelation of his own sin, a time of repentance and cleansing, and an open ear to hear the heart of God asking, "Whom shall I send? And who will go for us?" (Isa. 6:8). Out of pure worship there was an immediate and spontaneous response from Isaiah, "Here am I. Send me!" And God opened the floodgates of heaven to Isaiah and said, "Go and tell this people" (v. 9).

In a similar experience with God, Saul of Tarsus (later called Paul) had an encounter with God, for the first time in true worship, and heard the living Christ convincing him of sin and granting to him an assignment from heaven that would change the entire world forever (Acts 9:1-19).

Do you hear your own heart saying, as you worship, "Here am I. Send me!"? If not, return to Him in worship now. Sunday after Sunday are you hearing your church saying to God out of their worship, "Here we are. Send us!" If not, why not?

What would happen if more of God's people returned to true worship? What would happen in our world if all His children, globally, met God daily in true worship?

The Living Christ, revealed to John in Revelation, opened His heart to the seven churches of Asia Minor (Rev. 2–3), and pleaded with them to return to Him (Repent!). The church at Ephesus had left their first love and were about to lose everything. But Christ pled with them to "remember the height from which you have fallen! Repent and do the things you did at first" (Rev 2:5). Then Christ urged the church, "He who has an ear, let him hear what the Spirit says to the churches. To him who overcomes [remains faithful], I will give the right to eat from the tree of life, which is in the paradise of God" (Rev. 2:7).

What do you believe God could do to and through a church that returns to a full and true relationship with Him in worship and obedience? Explain.

_____

_____

_____

Today, so many of God's people and His churches are returning to true worship. They are encountering God fully, and they are hearing His voice, and their response is, "Here we are. Send us!" And God, out of their worship, is calling, sending, and using thousands around the world. May this be multiplied many times over!

Do you hear your own heart saying, as you worship, "Here am I. Send me!"? If not, return to Him in worship now. Sunday after Sunday are you hearing your church saying to God out of their worship, "Here we are. Send us!" If not, why not?

Day 2: Worship and the Early Church

God Himself has established the early church as a pattern for us all. This is why every generation, sooner or later, cries out from their hearts, "Let us return to the pattern seen in the early church. God, through them, turned their entire world upside down!" This is especially true of their worship. More came out of their worship times than any other time.

The believers in Jerusalem were literally born to worship. Jesus commanded them to stay together, in one place, until the Father sent the promised Holy Spirit. For days they met in prayer and with Scripture before God, obedient to their Lord. In God's presence, God poured out His Spirit upon every believer. It was not only a life-transforming moment but also a history-changing moment of God's choosing.

Read Acts 2:42-43. To what did those in the first church devote themselves?

_____

_____

_____

How would you define the experience of this first church?

_____

_____

_____

> They devoted themselves to the apostles' teaching and to the fellowship, to the breaking of bread and to prayer. Everyone was filled with awe, and many wonders and miraculous signs were done by the apostles.
>
> — Acts 2:42-43

Throughout history the people of God greatly used, and greatly changed, have had this same pattern: obediently, all together, in one place before God, until God poured out His Spirit upon them.

This early church worshiped daily—in prayer, songs, fellowship, teaching, and observing the Lord's Supper. Baptism occurred daily, and the fear of the Lord came upon every person. Through the leaders (apostles) God wrought great wonders among the people, and people were being saved daily. Daily worship was their pattern.

When persecution arose and their spiritual leaders were put in prison, God's people worshiped together in one place, praying together, and God

About noon the following day as they were on their journey and approaching the city, Peter went up on the roof to pray. He became hungry and wanted something to eat, and while the meal was being prepared, he fell into a trance. He saw heaven opened and something like a large sheet being let down to earth by its four corners.

— Acts 10:9-11

While Peter was still thinking about the vision, the Spirit said to him, "Simon, three men are looking for you. So get up and go downstairs. Do not hesitate to go with them, for I have sent them."

— Acts 10:19-20

moved again upon them all with great boldness and power (Acts 4). Each lived in worship daily, and God guided and empowered them all. After Peter had been praying on a housetop, God spoke clearly to him, resulting in the Gentiles hearing the gospel, beginning with Cornelius and all of his household. This was confirmed when Peter reported to a worshiping church in Jerusalem (Acts 10–11).

Read Acts 10:9-11 and Acts 10:19-20. Summarize how Peter's heart had become prepared to hear from God.

_____

_____

_____

What did Peter do that he would not have done without having been prepared by the Spirit?

_____

_____

_____

As Philip worshiped, the Spirit involved him and the church in Jerusalem in the great revival in Samaria. Later the Spirit guided him to the Ethiopian Eunuch, who took the gospel to northern Africa (Acts 8:4-5,26-38). A worshiping church stood in God's presence together daily. They heard from God and obeyed immediately. God was glorified through them daily, and His purposes to bring a world to Himself unfolded.

Day 3: Why Christians Gather

The gathering of God's people before God is their very life. The very word *church* means "called out and gathered together, an assembly, a congregation." When Jesus said that He would "build His church," He was announcing that His people would be a "gathered people," a community of faith.

They are a chosen people in a covenant relationship with Holy God. They are a royal priesthood (1 Pet. 2:9), and they are required by their nature to gather in His presence. As they gather, they will hear from God, for they are to be "Christ's ambassadors, as though God were making his appeal through us" (2 Cor. 5:20).

If God's people do not gather in pure worship before God, they will not adequately hear from God. Not to hear from God is for His people to be disoriented at the very heart of who they are, and they will soon "die" spiritually. Their very life comes from every word from God (Deut. 8:3; John 6:63).

When God was ready to inaugurate world redemption, His people were gathered together in an upper room, in prayer and the Word of God, being exhorted, taught, and led by the apostles. It was in their "gathering" that the Holy Spirit was poured out upon them, and everyone present was filled with the Holy Spirit. And everyone spoke the Word with boldness (Acts 2; 4).

It was also when they were gathered together, in worship, in Antioch, that God spoke to them all and told them to "set apart for me Barnabas and Saul for the work to which I have called them" (Acts 13:3). They heard God together and obeyed together, and God began His plan to take the gospel to the Gentiles. God could have done this some other way. He didn't. He did it through the gathered people of God, and this church met regularly in worship and prayer, to which Paul returned to report to them the mighty deeds of God among the Gentiles.

Read Acts 13:1-3. How many of the people who heard God speak probably foresaw the churches and converts that would result from that worship service?

_____

_____

_____

In the church at Antioch there were prophets and teachers: Barnabas, Simeon called Niger, Lucius of Cyrene, Manaen (who had been brought up with Herod the tetrarch) and Saul. While they were worshiping the Lord and fasting, the Holy Spirit said, "Set apart for me Barnabas and Saul for the work to which I have called them." So after they had fasted and prayed, they placed their hands on them and sent them off.

— Acts 13:1-3

When God's people worship together, God encounters them and speaks to His covenant people. There, together, God has made Himself known and done His greatest work.

Based on your knowledge of human nature, explain your answer.

_____

_____

_____

But it must be remembered, worship throughout the Bible, and to this very day, is the exclusive prerogative of God's people. Worship was designed by God for His covenant people. Only those in the covenant relationship can worship.

Worship was not designed for "lost" people. They cannot truly worship because they do not have a saving relationship with God. Therefore, God's people must worship. If "worship services" are turned into "evangelistic services," God's people will "die" for lack of worship. Evangelistic services will be planned for lost people, and God will bless. But *worship* as God's people gather is very specific with God!

If worship is made into an evangelistic service for lost people, God's people cannot worship, and ultimately the lost will go unreached. When God's people worship together, God encounters them and speaks to His covenant people. There, together, God has made Himself known and done His greatest work.

Would you plan worship for the purpose of God's people meeting their God as His covenant people?

_____

Explain.

_____

_____

_____

Do you think Christians know that worship is for them to meet as a covenant people with God?

_____

Do the "gathered people of God" experience new life from Him when they worship Him together?

_____

Is the result that God's people are equipped and inspired to share the gospel with the lost and seeking? Respond.

_____

_____

_____

_____

Day 4: Worship and Missions

Worship is the very life of missions. More happens for missions in individuals and churches in worship than at any other time. The heart of God is for the nations of the world (Matt. 28:18-20; Acts 1:8).

When God's people worship, God places a world on their hearts. In worship the Scriptures are shared, and the Spirit opens the minds and hearts of God's people to Truth; and Truth, who is Jesus Christ, is concerned with world redemption. The cross, so central to the Christian life, was for the world. Pentecost was to enable every believer to go into all the world and share God's good news with the nations.

As clearly as Abraham or Moses or Jeremiah or Paul encountered God and His heart for a lost world, so will God's people today experience God in their lives. I do not believe a church is truly worshiping if no one, or very few, are sensing God's call to missions. A self-centered church is not a worshiping church. They are just not encountering the God of Scripture. They may be practicing tradition, or religion, but not worship!

Read Revelation 3:14-17. How would you describe an "on-mission" church—one that contrasts with the description of the church at Laodicea?

_____

_____

_____

_____

"To the angel of the church in Laodicea write: These are the words of the Amen, the faithful and true witness, the ruler of God's creation. I know your deeds, that you are neither cold nor hot. I wish you were either one of the other! So, because you are lukewarm—neither hot nor cold—I am about to spit you out of my mouth. You say, 'I am rich; I have acquired wealth and do not need a thing.' But you do not realize that you are wretched, pitiful, poor, blind and naked."
— Revelation 3:14-17

Even Abraham, in worship, was assured: God said, "I will surely bless you and make your descendants as numerous as the stars in the sky and as the sand on the seashore. Your descendants will take possession of the cities of their enemies, and through your offspring all nations on earth will be blessed, because you have obeyed me" (Gen. 22:17-18).

Worship is an encounter with God where, for His name and glory, we release all there is of us (mind, heart, soul, and strength) to Him, as a loving and spontaneous act of worship. Out of that moment, the worshiper is "transformed by the renewing of your mind. Then you will be able to test and approve what God's will is—his good, pleasing and perfect will" (Rom. 12:1-2). That "good, pleasing and perfect will" of

God revealed in Scripture is holiness, by which we see God as He pursues the lost of the nations of the world.

So many of the testimonies of our missionaries tell of receiving clarifying commands and responding to God's call to missions in some moment of personal or corporate worship. I (Henry) watched, on one weekend at Ridgecrest Conference Center, more than one hundred couples respond to God's claim and call on their lives for ministry or missions. It came as we worshiped together for three days.

A "mission heart" was granted to the early church in Jerusalem, as they worshiped. The Spirit guided individuals, such as Philip, to go down to Samaria. A great revival broke out, and the church in Jerusalem sent Peter and John to see what God was doing and report back.

Revival spread through the towns and villages of Samaria. The church came to know the mind of God for the Samaritans (Acts 8:25). Immediately the Spirit sent Philip to an Ethiopian eunuch (Acts 8:26ff), and the gospel spread to North Africa. Soon, as Peter was worshiping, God opened the gospel to Cornelius and his household (Acts 10), and the gospel was now among the Gentiles. When Peter reported back to the gathered believers in Jerusalem (Acts 11:15-18), they saw the missionary heart of God to the world.

Read Acts 8:34-35, 38. Philip and the man from Ethiopia had a divine appointment. Philip was ready to share truth, and the Ethiopian was ready to receive truth. What was the result?

_____

_____

_____

As God's people gather in His presence, missions can be born afresh. Every church, as it gathers, ought to expect some touch of God for missions as they worship. An invitation may be in order for those being called to missions, regularly. It would be in keeping with the purposes of God in worship.

The eunuch asked Philip, "Tell me, please, who is the prophet talking about, himself or someone else?" Then Philip began with that very passage of Scripture and told him the good news about Jesus. . . . And he gave orders to stop the chariot. Then both Philip and the eunuch went down into the water and Philip baptized him.

— Acts 8:34-35, 38

In God's Word we come to "know the truth," and our lives can respond in total surrender to Jesus Christ as Lord. In that moment, true worship has taken place, and God is honored.

Day 5: Now It's Our Turn

Jesus said, strategically, "If you hold to my teaching, you are really my disciples. Then you will know the truth, and the truth will set you free" (John 8:31-32).

This is what this study has been all about: to help us abide in (live our lives in) God's Word. In God's Word we come to "know the truth," and our lives can respond in total surrender to Jesus Christ as Lord. In that moment, true worship has taken place, and God is honored. Great glory comes to Him as, unhindered, He reveals Himself in us and through us to a watching world.

But all is meaningless—even blasphemous—if we hear and understand, and even verbally agree to all God says, but we do nothing to obey God's commands. This is especially true about personal and corporate worship.

First, what must we do to obey God in personal worship?

1. Each Christian must choose to live a lifestyle of worship, knowing that as a child of God, all of life is "holy ground." Christians must "ask, seek, and knock" (Matt. 7:7-8) as a way of life. God is seeking such persons before Him.

2. A Christian must anticipate fresh encounters with God constantly. Every time a Christian opens the Scripture, he is face-to-face with God, the Author. The Holy Spirit actively works to "teach you all things and will remind you of everything I have said to you" (John 14:26; 16:13).

Christians should approach the Scripture in an attitude of worship, expecting to be totally available to God, for His glory. And they should expect never to be the same again.

Each believer must pray, expecting a full encounter with God in worship. To approach God in prayer is to enter "the Most Holy Place" (Heb. 10:19), where all we are and have is presented to God, for His glory. Out of such an encounter God will express Himself and His will, and the transformation of life will be obvious.

A believer must seek the enabling of the Holy Spirit for all of his or her life. The Holy Spirit is God's enabler in worship (John 16:14-15). The Spirit brings one face-to-face with God and brings the Person of Jesus into full lordship. No one will call Jesus Lord, or know Him as Lord, without the Spirit (1 Cor. 12:13).

3. A true worshiper must know the voice of God and know when He is speaking. To miss His voice in worship is to miss true worship.

4. A Christian must come to worship with a heart and life

committed to obey God out of every encounter. This is a choice ahead of time. Worship is never complete without obedience, so an obedient heart is essential to true worship.

Second, what must we do to obey God in corporate worship?

1. We must choose to be with God's people, as a way of life. When God's people gather before God, and when God's people gather in a home, the body is in worship. When God's people gather in the workplace, the body is in worship. When God's people gather in their church building, they are worshiping (prayer meeting, business meeting, Sundays, special times). But sometimes the broader gathering of God's people may occur in a citywide, or area-wide meeting. This time of worship is crucial to experience a special kind of encounter with God. Often, it is in such kingdom meetings that life-changing decisions of obedience take place.

2. God's people must choose not to forsake "the assembling of ourselves together," before God (Heb. 10:25). Each gathering holds infinite potential with God. But God is honored when His people choose to meet before Him in worship.

3. Each person must be an active seeker after God, when Christians meet in corporate worship. No true worshiper can be passive when worshiping with others. God does things with His people corporately that He does not do individually. So each worshiper should expect eternity encounters with God in the body as they worship. Most of the significant decisions in our lives have come out of corporate worship. But we were seeking Him there!

4. Each worshiper, exposed so thoroughly to God's presence in corporate worship (singing, prayer, Scriptures, *koinonia*) must come with a commitment to obey God's commands. Each must have a heart that is ready with, "Yes, Lord!" even before God speaks, and "Here am I; send me!" even before He calls His commands.

Review the four steps of obedience in corporate worship listed above. How could a change in your heart for worship affect other worshipers?

_____

_____

_____

_____

The church by nature is a gathered people of God. Not to gather together is fatal to a church. For a church by essence is a worshiping people.

I rejoiced with those who said to me, "Let us go to the house of the Lord."

— Psalm 122:1

If you were being truly obedient to God in worship, in what ways could you demonstrate your repentant commitment to godly, humble, awestruck, praising, prayerful worship?

_____

_____

_____

Every generation of the people of God met God in life-transforming worship. God worked mightily through them to change their world, and bring glory to Himself. A transformed life that comes out of true worship is the greatest testimony there is for a watching world. Surely our generation needs to see and experience a worshiping people of God and be changed themselves. Surely God is worthy of the finest worship of which we are capable. May great glory come to Him from our generation as we truly worship Him!

Group Leader Guide

This group study guide includes: group leader ideas, introductory session plans, and weekly group session plans.

Who? A group study of *Worship: Believers Experiencing God* is preferably led by the pastor because worship is so central to the life of the church. Ideally, this should also be an ongoing study for new believers joining the church. The interactive study of this book by individuals on a daily basis will immerse learners in the Scripture's teachings about worship. Regular use of the resource by every person involved in the study also will prepare them to reflect, discuss, and apply what they are learning as they interact with one another about the content during group sessions.

Where? This resource and topic can be processed each week over coffee, during a discussion time in a variety of settings, or in a church sanctuary as whole congregations learn and grow together in making their worship more focused on God.

When? Select a time that works for your particular group. The plans for the sessions aim for about an hour of discussion and prayer. However, allow the Holy Spirit to determine your schedule and guide the process of the study.

How? The plans in this section serve as a framework on which to build your preparation for guiding the group study. Your goal should be to offer the topic, teaching, and time to God for His direction. Before each session, as a leader or group member, please:

- Pray for each group member.
- Study the part of the study the group will discuss.
- Encourage others in the group to maintain their personal processing of the material.
- Get in touch right away with anyone who misses a session.

Introductory Session

Before the Session

• Promote the study. Secure a place where the number of people you expect can be comfortable and participate in discussion. Have enough copies of this book for each individual expected plus others who may be unexpected or join the study during later.

• Read and process the entire book. It will be easier to see how God is guiding your group if you are familiar with what they will be studying.

During the Session

• Begin on time. Make latecomers welcome with as little interruption as possible. Provide nametags. Even if an entire congregation is the study group, discussion will be helped if people can call each other by name. It will also make anyone new who has come for this study feel at less of a disadvantage and help the group feel connected. Welcome the group.

• Say, "The purpose of this study is to help a church come to unity of heart and life in their understanding and experience of God's requirements and standards for worship." Read Romans 12:1-2.

• Ask the group, "What does the Scripture say that spiritual worship is?" If needed, refer them back to Romans 12:1. Discuss ways and attitudes that could be examples of living sacrifices, holy and pleasing to God.

• Ask, "According to Scripture, what is the process by which we are to be transformed?" Romans 12:2 contains this reference. Invite the group to discuss examples of people they know whom the Lord has transformed. Encourage them to think of worship services that were part of the transformation experiences.

• Say, "Some congregations struggle with how to worship. If people think 'how to worship' means style of music, time of services, length of preaching, and who takes the offering, think about how that could distract them from focusing on God's mercy, offering their bodies as living sacrifices, and being holy and pleasing to God." Ask the group to apply Romans 12:1, discussing what could help worship be scriptural.

• Use this outline: Genuine worship is always transformational. Nothing is higher on God's agenda for Himself and His people than true worship. It is also true that nothing is higher on Satan's agenda than to: (1) Deceive God's people. Read Revelation 12:9. (2) Create substitutes for true worship. (3) Distort and change true worship.

As Jesus shows us in Matthew 4:1-11, when Satan tempted Him, the only sure way of dealing with this deception is Scripture.

Therefore, I urge you, brothers, in view of God's mercy, to offer your bodies as living sacrifices, holy and pleasing to God—which is your spiritual act of worship. Do not conform any longer to the pattern of this world, but be transformed by the renewing of your mind. Then you will be able to test and approve what God's will is—his good, pleasing and perfect will.

— Romans 12:1-2

Ask, "How did Jesus use Scripture to deal with Satan's desire to deceive Him?" Discuss and make a list on a tear sheet, chalk or dry board, or an overhead cell, of the group's comments.

- Review the comments and/or say that some of Satan's deceptions may include: (1) the traditions of men, (2) the words of men, (3) the persuasions of men, (4) the pleading of men, (5) the perpetuated fads of men, (6) the allure of popularity with men.
- Say, "God has always guided His people by a clear Word of revelation. Satan has always twisted and distorted God's Word. However, God's Holy Spirit is always present in His people to correct all they are confronting and bring everything into harmony with God's Word. Let's proceed in the confidence that God will guide us into all truth as we learn more about worshiping Him in the truth of His Word."
- Outline the topics for the six-week study using the contents page.
- Distribute books to those who have not already obtained their books.
- Dismiss with prayer.

Week One: What God Did in Creation

Before the Session

- Pray for each group member. Study "Week One: What God Did in Creation." Encourage others to maintain their personal processing of the material and get in touch with anyone who missed the last session.

During the Session

- Welcome the group. Say: "Have you observed that God has placed the need and desire to worship into human nature? If we were to go anywhere on earth, even to the most remote places people live, we would find human beings worshiping a god or gods. Why is this? The answer would appear to be that this is the way God created us. Each of us worships something or someone—whatever is most important to us, what or who we value the most. If we define worship as being that which we will 'bow' to, by giving our allegiance, our interest, time, and affection, what have you observed people worshiping?" Discuss.

  Read Matthew 6:21. Ask, "In light of our discussion, how does this verse fit? If an unseen observer watched your life for a month, what or whom do you think the observer would conclude is the object of your worship?" Ask the group to keep this in mind throughout the study.

- Say: "When Paul referred to God in Romans 1:9 as, 'God, whom I serve with my whole heart' ('with my spirit' in some translations), the word translated "serve" is the Greek word *latreuo*, which can also be

For where your treasure is, there your heart will be also.

— Matthew 6:21

translated as meaning "worship." In other words Paul's ministry itself was a form of worship. It was not something he did because he felt he had to; it was something he did out of love for his Lord." Ask: "Do you actively worship God with your whole heart as you live out the truth of the gospel in your daily life? Give some examples." Discuss the responses as you list them on paper, a board, or overhead cell.

- Ask, "How were you affected by the God-focus rating in day 1 (p. 16)? Which question most captured your attention? Discuss.

- Ask the group what they learned about the Hebrew word for worship, *shachah* (pp. 21-22). Responses should pick up on the fact that it often presents a picture of someone bowing, kneeling, or prostrating himself before God. Ask, "Do you have a *shachah* heart? Explain."

- Say, "In the Old Testament, the only access God's people had to the Holy of Holies—a place heavily curtained, set apart, and where God's presence dwelt—was through the high priest. He could enter only once a year on the Day of Atonement to make a sacrifice on behalf of the people. But through the sacrifice of Christ for our sins, believers have entered a new covenant with God." Read Hebrews 10:19-22.

> Ask, "What makes the worship of all believers acceptable to God in a way that could not have been accepted under the Old Covenant?" Discuss the answers. Discuss what it means for God to allow believers to come before His holiness. How would a strong awareness of being in God's presence affect the way believers worship?

- Invite members to share briefly about the time when they consciously repented of their sins and invited Jesus to come into their lives. As leader, you might start the sharing. After several have spoken, remind them that according to Psalm 51:17, God accepts the offering of a broken and repentant heart. With this in mind, how should believers prepare to worship in a way that will be acceptable to God? (See p. 34.)

- Close with prayer for God to convict and cleanse the group of their sins and prepare their hearts for the next time they gather to worship.

Week Two: Why God Is So Central in Worship

Before the Session

- Pray for group members. Study "Week Two: Why Is God So Central in Worship?" Encourage others to maintain their personal processing of the material and get in touch with anyone who missed the last session.

- Have some paper, a chalk or dry marker board, or overhead cel ready to list group comments and answers.

Therefore, brothers, since we have confidence to enter the Most Holy Place by the blood of Jesus, by a new and living way opened for us through the curtain, that is, his body, and since we have a great priest over the house of God, let us draw near to God with a sincere heart in full assurance of faith, having our hearts sprinkled to cleanse us from a guilty conscience and having our bodies washed with pure water.

— Hebrews 10:19-22

The sacrifices of God are a broken spirit; a broken and contrite heart, O God, you will not despise.

— Psalm 51:17

During the Session

- Welcome the group and invite them to contribute to making a list of the Ten Commandments. If necessary, they can refer to Exodus 20:1-17. Point out that the first four commandments deal with our relationship with God. The remaining six detail how, if we are in relationship with God, we are to relate to other people. Reflecting on the key verse (p. 35) and the material in week two, how did Jesus summarize all the commandments for the scribes when they asked him which commandment was most important? Discuss.

- Ask the group how the holiness of God should affect their worship, their lives, and their involvement at church (p. 37)? How have they found any of these ideas to be real in their lives? Discuss.

- Ask someone in the group to read aloud Luke 6:32-36. Say, "This passage reveals a command that some believers may feel justified in ignoring. After hearing these words, who are people presuming to be the greater authority if they decide not to show kindness or mercy to someone—they or God? Why?" Discuss. (See p. 38.)

- Point out that in order to be acceptable to God, we must repent of those things that are opposite of His nature and His commands. If we are to be right with God, then we must have things right with others. Matthew 5:23-24 tells us that God, to whose nature we have been reconciled, requires us to be reconciled to our brothers before our worship is acceptable to Him: "Therefore, if you are offering your gift at the altar and there remember that your brother has something against you, leave your gift there in front of the altar. First go and be reconciled to your brother; then come and offer your gift."

  Ask, "If an individual who knows something being held against him by someone must go take care of it to be acceptable to God in worship, what, then, would be some similar barriers to the worship of a congregation being acceptable to God? What would it take to remove such barriers? How are humility and repentance connected, both in reconciling with others and with God?" Discuss. (See p. 40.)

- Say, "God's name is who God is, His essential nature. God never acts contrary to His nature. To call Him Lord and then live or act contrary to His name is to blaspheme His name. That would be taking His name in vain and breaking the Third Commandment. When God's people do not reflect God's character, it causes believers to stumble in their walk and keeps unbelievers from seeing the truth of God, based on the false testimony of believers who misuse God's name."

  Ask, "If believers are going to join God in redeeming a lost world,

"If you love those who love you, what credit is that is to you? Even 'sinners' love those who love them. And if you do good to those who are good to you, what credit is that to you? Even 'sinners' do that. And if you lend to those from whom you expect repayment, what credit is that to you? Even 'sinners' lend to 'sinners' expecting to be repaid in full. But love your enemies, do good to them, and lend to them without expecting to get anything back. Then your reward will be great, and you will be sons of the Most High, because he is kind to the ungrateful and wicked. Be merciful, just as your Father is merciful."

— Luke 6:32-36

why must believers constantly commit themselves to allowing God to change the way they speak, behave, and act?" Discuss. (See p. 45.)

- Ask, "How can the sabbath be a sign between God and His chosen people, that He has redeemed them and sanctified them for Himself forever?" Read Exodus 31:13-17 to clarify. Discuss. (See p. 46.)

- Ask, "What are some ways we can observe the sabbath to give God greater honor? What are some of the most God-honoring actions taking place around you on any given Sunday?" Discuss.

- Close with prayer asking God to transform the group into reconcilers, who are also loving and merciful in the selfless ways that God has been loving and merciful to them.

Week Three: What Is God's Standard for Acceptable Worship?

Before the Session

- Pray for group members. Study "Week Three: What Is God's Standard for Acceptable Worship?" Encourage the group to continue to process the material. Get in touch with anyone who missed the last session.

- Have some paper, a chalk or dry marker board, or overhead cel ready to list group comments and answers.

During the Session

- Welcome the group by quoting the week's Scripture-memory verse, Romans 12:1 (p. 53). Ask, "Why does God require a sacrifice?" Lead the group in discussing how God's plan of redemption always required a sacrifice, the shedding of blood. (See pp. 53-54.)

- Review "The Progression of Redemption" (p. 54): (1) A lamb for a man, (2) A lamb for a family, (3) A lamb for a nation, (4) The Lamb for the world.

  Ask the group to reflect on how God prepared His people across the centuries to receive the sacrifice of Jesus. Then ask them to think of how they could express in their own words how the Lamb slain for the world also satisfies the necessary sacrifice for each of them individually. Invite group members to share some of their thoughts. (See p. 56.)

  Because this is at the very basis of why we come together to worship God, our Creator and Savior, next ask them to share their understanding of this with one or two of the people nearest to them. When they have finished, challenge them to share their explanation with at least one other person in the next 24 hours.

Therefore, I urge you, brothers, in view of God's mercy, to offer your bodies as living sacrifices, holy and pleasing to God—this is your spiritual act of worship.

— Romans 12:1

- Say: "Because Christ made the ultimate sacrifice with His blood, God looks to those redeemed by that sacrifice to make spiritual sacrifices." Read 1 Peter 2:5. Say, "Let's discuss how believers' lives are like living stones, being built into a spiritual house, becoming a holy priesthood, offering up spiritual sacrifices. As part of the body of Christ, you have become part of God's family. Each believer can make intercession for himself or anyone else before God. Each believer functions as an individual priest, relating directly to God, and the sacrifices God's priesthood offers no longer require that any blood be shed. What God looks for as an offering is a ready and loving heart." Discuss. (See pp. 57-58.)

- Say, "God's Word tells us that because of Jesus' sacrifice, the worshiper now also becomes the worship sacrifice. God waits for us to place ourselves on the altar." Ask the group to identify and define the five admonitions Paul gives in Romans 12:1-2. These are found in day 3 (pp. 62-64). Write the group's responses. (1) The sacrifice we make will be a complete one. (2) The sacrifice we make will be a living one. (3) The sacrifice we make will be a holy one. (4) The sacrifice we make will be an acceptable one. (5) The sacrifice we make will be a transforming one. Discuss statements from the group to explain each of the five items.

- Read Luke 6:38. Say, "Worship is an offering; it is an act of giving. It will mean the gift of time. The person who worships sports will give both time and money to fulfill his desire to worship. A person who worships a boat or a car will give all the time and money needed to fulfill that need to worship. Those who worship a career and money will give all the time and effort needed to get what they want. Giving is at the heart of worship."

  Ask the group, "When it comes to worshiping God, is that how you feel? Do you go to church looking forward to joining other worshipers in the offering of yourself to God in worship, or do you go, like many seem to do, think only of what you will get or how much you will enjoy yourself?" Invite the group to discuss their thoughts on being givers or getters when it comes to worship. In light of this study, what are some of their thoughts about "shopping" for a church? (See p. 66.)

- Remind the group of Jesus' words in Luke 6:38. Ask, "What if God were to lead you to a church that humanly speaking would not be your first choice but God had chosen to put you for His purposes? What if the music of this church was not your preference? Or something else could be changed to be more to your liking? What would you do?" Discuss. (See p. 67.)

You also, like living stones, are being built into a spiritual house to be a holy priesthood, offering spiritual sacrifices acceptable to God through Jesus Christ.

— 1 Peter 2:5

Give, and it will be given to you. A good measure, pressed down, shaken together and running over, will be poured into your lap. For with the measure you use, it will be measured to you.

— Luke 6:38

Search me, O God, and know my heart; test me and know my anxious thoughts. See if there is any offensive way in me, and lead me in the way everlasting.

— Psalm 139:23-24

- Read Psalm 139:23-24 aloud. Say, "Our attitudes determine whether God looks with favor on what we bring to Him in worship. We are the worshipers, not only those leading in worship." (See p. 69.)
- Close with prayer, asking God to do a cleansing work in each heart to make the group's worship more acceptable to Him, the very most any believer truly desires to "get" from worship.

Week Four: The Lifestyle of a Transformed Worshiper

Before the Session

- Pray for each group member. Study "Week Four: The Lifestyle of a Transformed Worshiper." Encourage the group to continue processing to the material. Get in touch with anyone who missed the last session.

- Have some paper, a chalk or dry marker board, or overhead cel ready to list group comments and answers.

During the Session

- Welcome the group by quoting the week's key verse, 2 Corinthians 3:18 (p. 71). Ask, "Just from what this verse says, what are some things that can be said of someone who is being transformed?" Discuss.

  Say, "Being transformed is something we are to experience the Holy Spirit doing in our lives. The result of a transformed life is to have Jesus' life expressing itself through us. John 14:6 says that Jesus described Himself as "the way and the truth and the life." Persons transformed by the Holy Spirit will be like Jesus in that they will know the way of salvation Jesus has provided. They have the truth of Jesus evident in their lives. And they know that eternal life changes a believer's perspective about earthly things to focus on eternal things."

And we, who with unveiled faces all reflect the Lord's glory, are being transformed into his likeness with ever-increasing glory, which comes from the Lord, who is the Spirit.

— 2 Corinthians 3:18

- Ask the group to compile a list of people who do not know Jesus. (See p. 72.) Write down the names as they're said. Then ask, "How open are you to Christ's speaking through you? Do you have a lifestyle of worship that would allow Christ's influence to be seen? If someone who doesn't know Jesus came to a worship service with you, what are some ways that one could see Jesus reflected there?" Discuss. (See p. 73.)
- Say, "Mary gives us an incredible example of a worshipful heart. Others doubted that what she had done was appropriate." Read Matthew 26:13. Ask, "How could we begin to capture that same attitude of worship when we gather in God's presence?" Discuss. (See pp. 73-76.)

"I tell you the truth, wherever this gospel is preached throughout the world, what she has done will also be told, in memory of her."

— Matthew 26:13

- Review the examples of worship at home shared in day 2 (p. 77). Allow the group to recall what the study reported about Timothy, Abram, Isaac, and Jacob. Ask the group to discuss ways worship can be made a vital part of Christian homes. How could God change people in our households through worship experiences there? Discuss.

- Ask volunteers to read the descriptions of how God used homes in Acts 16:24-36; Acts 9:36-42; Acts 16:11-15; and Romans 16:3. Discuss the impact these examples had on the kingdom of God. (See p. 78.)

- Say, "Worship takes place in God's presence. Any encounter with God can involve our worship as He reveals His will and calls us to obey Him." Ask the group to pause a moment to reflect and pray, asking God to help them remember ways He has shown Himself to them and invited them to join Him in His work. Invite the group to share what has come to mind as a means of encouraging one another about how God uses a lifestyle of worship in transformed lives to accomplish His purposes.

- Say: "A dimension of worship that we seem to have lost today is worship of God by a nation. The examples in our study (pp. 81-83) are of God's people, the nation of Israel, gathering. As God's people today, when our congregation comes together, how could we emphasize the sense that we gather by the command of God, coming with preparation to be ready and worthy to worship, bringing our households to seek God's face and trust Him for His blessing?" Discuss.

- Say, "List three possible results in our community that could take place if we shared that same heart with other groups of God's people." Revival should surface as a result, not a scheduled activity.

- Remind the group that Paul was a worshiper. He often referenced his own worship as well as teaching and encouraging the churches about worship. As goes the worship of spiritual leaders, so goes the worship of God's people. Since this is a biblical pattern, how important is it that believers lift up their spiritual leaders and encourage them in keeping and celebrating the covenant God has made with His people? What are some practical ways to be sure believers never overlook the well-being and spiritual health of their leaders? Discuss. (See pp. 85-87.)

- Close with prayer for each member of the group, praying that as spiritual leaders to their households, their spouses, their congregation, their workplace, they have an awesome responsibility and privilege to walk with the Lord and reveal His glory to a dying world.

Week Five: Heaven's Pattern for Worship

Before the Session

- Pray for each group member. Study "Week Five: Heaven's Pattern for Worship." Encourage others in the group to maintain their personal study. Get in touch with anyone who missed the last session.

- Have some paper, a chalk or dry marker board, or overhead cel ready to list group comments and answers.

During the Session

- Ask the group to join you in a prayer of praise, using this week's key verse, Revelation 4:11 (p. 89). Say: "Have you considered the importance of God's glory in worship? Both the Old and New Testaments have many references to God's glory. This week's study presented two aspects of God's glory: the glory of God's presence in worship and the glory God is due in worship. (See pp. 91-95.) The glory of God's presence reveals both God's nature and our sin. It purifies us by calling us to repent and makes our worship acceptable to Him by cleansing and filling us with His power."

- Ask: "Are you experiencing the glory of God in personal and corporate worship? Do you feel aware of worshiping a holy, awesome, and powerful God?" Invite the group to discuss with examples. (See p. 93.)

- Say: "Many Scriptures remind us that God is the only One who is worthy of worship. He makes clear that no glory is to go to any other." Read Isaiah 42:8. Ask: "What are some ways glory can be taken from the Lord in worship? Why is it that for true worship to take place, God must be the focus and not the talent, ability, or presence of any human?" Discuss. Point out that God makes talent and ability, to reveal His glory and not substitute for it. (See p. 94.)

- Remind the group that Matthew 10:29 says, "Are not two sparrows sold for a penny? Yet not one of them will fall to the ground apart from the will of your Father." Say: "The God we worship has absolute authority and complete sovereignty over all things. This includes you and me. Nothing ever happens that is beyond His control." Ask, "If we really were to grasp this, what difference would it make in all of our daily reactions to life?" Discuss the group's responses. (See pp. 96-98.)

- Say: "It is impossible for the human mind to understand the things of God. We must depend on God to help us grasp something of the magnitude of who He is. Who we understand Him to be directly affects how we approach Him in worship. We can be encouraged, knowing we have God's Holy Spirit living in us to guide us." (See p. 99.)

  Ask the group to turn to one or two others and discuss this statement: Explain what it means to have the Holy Spirit help you understand more of who God is. After a few minutes invite volunteers to summarize some of the thoughts they have been discussing.

You are worthy, our Lord and God, to receive glory and honor and power, for you created all things, and by your will they were created and have their being.

— Revelation 4:11

- Say: "God is eternal, and He has made it possible for believers to be eternally free from sin and guilt. We can be free from any bondage to the past, forever. The blood of Christ cleanses us from all sin."

  Ask: "What are you free to do since Christ has freed you from the past and guilt? Are you free to forgive? free to trust? free to love?" (See p.101.) Invite the group to explain and discuss their responses. Conclude this part of the session by quoting Deuteronomy 33:27. "The eternal God is your refuge, and underneath are the everlasting arms."

- Read Revelation 4:11 again. Say, "When we worship here on earth, we are acknowledging God's activity in creation. Our bodies contain about 10 trillion cells, each cell having 100,000 genes that make up a unique genetic code for every single human being that ever has, does, or will live. His creative power is as mind-boggling as His eternity." (See pp. 105-107.)

  Ask the group: "Why is it the more we know about God's creation, the less in awe we seem to be of the Creator? Can we really offer God the worship He deserves if we no longer 'wonder'?"

  Say: "Close your eyes and ask yourselves, 'Have I lost the wonder? Is my worship motivated at all by the greatness of the God of creation?'"

  Allow time for some private prayer if the Spirit leads you.

- Ask, "If you are a believer who is aware of God's nature as One who is eternal, the Creator of infinite complexities, and our Redeemer, what connection should there be between the way you worship on Sunday mornings and how you live all week long?" Discuss.

- Pray that members will serve the Lord in word and deed, in worship with other believers and in their personal worship and daily lives.

Week Six: What Would Happen If We Returned to Worship?

Before the Session

- Pray for the group. Study "Week Six: What Would Happen If We Returned to Worship?" Encourage members to continue to process the material. Get in touch with anyone who missed the last session.

- Have some paper, a chalk or dry marker board, or overhead cel ready to list group comments and answers.

During the Session

- Welcome the group and say: "Not only does the action of worship presuppose a relationship with God, but it also presupposes that those taking part are worshipers. Though we were created to worship, do we nurture that ability in private so that we can express in public, with other believers, the relationship that has been growing in private?" Discuss and record some of the group's thoughts on paper, board, or overhead cel. (See p. 113.)

- Read Psalm 122:1. Ask: "Do you think of worship the way David did, with gladness? with the sense that in worship is where you want to be and know you belong?" Explain and discuss. (See p. 113.)

- Read Hebrews 10:25. Say: "Many believers do not even speak to, much less encourage, one another in worship. Others have simply stopped attending worship altogether. This is contrary to God's desire for deepening relationship with and through His people." (See p. 114.)

Ask them to discuss how even the most thoughtfully planned worship would be affected by people who show their love for God and one another through their attitudes and actions during worship. Brainstorm examples of an attitude and relationship checklist for worshipers in love with God. Say: "God reveals Himself to His people, and there is so much He would reveal if they would return to Him. It is God's ultimate desire that none should be lost or ruined by sin."

Read Ezekiel 18:30-32. Ask the group: "How does this Old Testament appeal to God's people impact your heart as you think of God's great compassion for us? How could deep love be communicated in worship and by worshipers?" Discuss. (See p. 115.)

- Say: "Often God waits to give an assignment to His people because He has promised to be available to them before a watching world. But if God's people do not gather in His presence with a heart to meet and hear Him, how can they respond? When you gather for worship, is it with the sense that God wants to remind the congregation of His assignment to be witnesses to His love and purpose?" Discuss.

- Ask, "What do you believe God could do to and through a church that returns to a full and true relationship with God in worship and obedience?" Create a list from the discussion. After a few moments, ask the group if this list could reflect the future for their congregation. Discuss. (See p. 118.)

- Say: "The early church is a pattern for us. (See pp. 119-120.) They not only heard and responded to the gospel, but they also turned the world upside down."

Read Acts 2:42: "They devoted themselves to the apostles' teaching and to the fellowship, to the breaking of bread and to prayer."

Ask, "What elements in our congregation reflect these simple

I rejoiced with those who said to me, "Let us go to the house of the Lord."
— Psalm 122:1

Let us not give up meeting together, as some are in the habit of doing, but let us encourage one another—and all the more as you see the Day approaching.
— Hebrews 10:25

actions by the early church?" List the responses. After writing several responses, ask the group to evaluate where, from looking at what they listed, someone might see the congregation's strength. Next ask which areas could use strengthening, according to what was listed. Name some simple actions that could grow the church in those weaker areas.

- Read Acts 13:1-3. Ask, "How many who heard God speak foresaw the millions of believers and churches that would result from that one worship service where they laid hands on Barnabas and Saul (most often referred to as Paul)? Do you ever think of the eternal potential of any of the worship services you attend?" Discuss. (See p. 121.)

- Say: "This history-changing event of setting apart Barnabas and Saul occurred in the setting of God's covenant people gathering to worship Him together. He equipped, inspired, and commissioned them to serve him. Knowing this can impact the importance we assign to gathering to worship. As a result of worship, do you see God's people leaving the gathering equipped and inspired to share the gospel with the lost and seeking? Do they realize that the intention for the gathering was for that to happen?" Discuss in the group. (See p. 123.)

- Say, "The church at Laodicea received harsh words in Revelation."
  Read Revelation 3:17. Ask, "In contrast to the back-slidden congregation at Laodicea, how would you describe an on-mission church by contrast?" Again, write down what the group lists as describing an on-mission church. Ask, "How could we better match that description in our church?" Discuss. (See p. 124.)

- Review the steps of obedience in day 5 of week six (pp. 126-128). Allow discussion. Ask, "If you were being truly obedient to God in worship, in what ways could you demonstrate your repentant commitment to godly, humble, awestruck, praising, prayerful, worship." Discuss.

- Say: "Every generation of the people of God met God in life-transforming worship. God worked mightily through them to change their world, and bring glory to Himself. A transformed life that comes out of true worship is the greatest testimony there is for a watching world. Surely our generation needs to see and experience a worshiping people of God and be changed themselves. Surely God is worthy of the deepest worship of which we are capable. May great glory come to Him from our generation as we truly worship Him!"

- Dismiss the session with a prayer, commissioning the group members to implement all they have learned about experiencing God in the worship of adoration and of service.

In the church at Antioch there were prophets and teachers: Barnabas, Simeon called Niger, Lucius of Cyrene, Manaen (who had been brought up with Herod the tetrarch) and Saul. While they were worshiping the Lord and fasting, the Holy Spirit said, "Set apart for me Barnabas and Saul for the work which I have called them." So after they had fasted and prayed, they place their hands on them and sent them off.

— Acts 13:1-3

Scripture Index

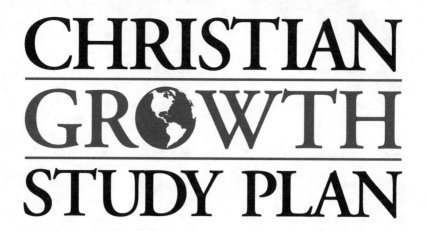

CHRISTIAN GROWTH STUDY PLAN

In the **Christian Growth Study Plan (formerly Church Study Course),** this book *Worship: Believers Experiencing God* is a resource for course credit in two Leadership and Skill Development diploma plans and one Christian Growth course. To receive credit, read the book, complete the learning activities, show your work to your pastor, a staff member or church leader, then complete the following information. This page may be duplicated. Send the completed page to:

Christian Growth Study Plan
127 Ninth Avenue, North
Nashville, TN 37234-0117
FAX: (615)251-5067
Email: cgspnet@lifeway.com

For information about the Christian Growth Study Plan, refer to the current Christian Growth Study Plan Catalog. Your church office may have a copy. If not, request a free copy from the Christian Growth Study Plan office (615/251-2525). Also available online at www.lifeway.com/cgsp/catalog.

COURSE CREDIT INFORMATION

Please check the appropriate box indicating the courses you want to apply this credit. You may check more than one.

❑ Church Growth and the Pastor (LS-0082)
❑ The Music Ministry (LS-0094)
❑ Worship (CG-0680)

PARTICIPANT INFORMATION

Rev. 3-01

Social Security Number (USA Only-optional)	Personal CGSP Number*	Date of Birth (Mo., Day, Yr.)

Name (First, MI, Last)	Home Phone

Address (Street, Route, or P.O. Box)	City, State, or Province	Zip/Postal Code

CHURCH INFORMATION

Church Name

Address (Street, Route, or P.O. Box)	City, State, or Province	Zip/Postal Code

CHANGE REQUEST ONLY

❑Former Name

❑Former Address	City, State, or Province	Zip/Postal Code

❑Former Church	City, State, or Province	Zip/Postal Code

Signature of Pastor, Conference Leader, or Other Church Leader	Date

*New participants are requested but not required to give SS# and date of birth. Existing participants, please give CGSP# when using SS# for the first time. Thereafter, only one ID# is required. *Mail To:* Christian Growth Study Plan, 127 Ninth Ave., North, Nashville, TN 37234-0117. Fax: (615)251-5067.